Series of Basic Information of Tibet of China

Tibetan Religions

GA ZANGJIA

CHINA INTERCONTINENTAL PRESS

图书在版编目(CIP)数据

西藏宗教／尕藏加.—北京：五洲传播出版社，
2003.6
（中国西藏基本情况）
ISBN 7-5085-0232-9

Ⅰ.西… Ⅱ.尕… Ⅲ.宗教史—西藏—英文
Ⅳ.B929.2

中国版本图书馆 CIP 数据核字（2003）第 041529 号

《中国西藏基本情况丛书》

主　　编：郭长建　　宋坚之
副 主 编：雷　珈
责任编辑：荆孝敏　　徐醒生
摄　　影：土　登　　车　刚　　杜泽泉　　陈宗烈
　　　　　　张　鹰　　赵远志　　唐召明等
版式设计：杨　津
制版印刷：深圳麟德电脑设计制作有限公司

中国西藏基本情况丛书—西藏宗教
（英文版）
翻　　译：左艳丽

五洲传播出版社
地址：中国北京北三环中路 31 号　邮编：100088
电话：82008174　网址：www.cicc.org.cn

开本：140 × 210　1/32　印张：6
2003 年 9 月第一版　印数：1-11500
ISBN 7-5085-0232-9/B·01
定价：38.00 元

CONTENTS

The Potala Palace.

Introduction

In order to understand Tibetan religious practices, it is necessary to begin with the Bon religion, for it is an indigenous religion of the Qinghai-Tibet Plateau enriched with regional and cultural characteristics. As an orthodox religious culture in Tibetan areas before the spread of Buddhism, the Bon religion was an important component of Tibetan traditional culture. Originating in remote antiquity, it underwent all the historical courses that ancient Tibetan society followed, and, consequently, advanced the civilization of Tibetan society in its early stages. At the same time, the Bon religion, claiming broad mass foundation, played an indispensable role in the later development of Tibetan Buddhism. For instance, Tibetan Buddhism absorbed many aspects of Bon, such as religious rituals and Buddhist guardian deities. Undeniably, the impact of Tibetan Buddhism on the Bon religion was powerful, even destructive. "With Buddhism spreading into the Tibetan areas continuously, the high prestige the Bon religion had once held among Tibetans was challenged and declined gradually, and, in the end, its orthodox position was replaced by Buddhism. From then on, the Bon religion began to collapse and had to retreat to certain remote areas to preserve its minor influence.

Therefore, throughout the Tibetan areas, except for a few remote districts, it is difficult to detect today the existence of the pure Bon religion." However, as the oldest culture aspect on the Qinghai-Tibet Plateau, the Bon religion is still survives with great vitality.

The origination, formation and development of Tibetan Buddhism maintained innumerable ties with the historical process and culture evolution of Indian Buddhism. In a rather exaggerated way, Tibetan Buddhism is a "production" of the religious culture transplanted to the Qinghai-Tibetan Plateau from Indian Buddhism. Meanwhile, during its course of formation and development, Tibetan Buddhism was once influenced greatly by traditional Tibetan culture, especially the Bon religion. It was the theoretical structures and ideological modes of the Bon religion that Tibetan Buddhism once adopted in the process of receiving or digesting the Buddhist culture emanating from India. Therefore, Tibetan Buddhism distinguished itself from other Buddhist branches by its plateau characteristics, which lay in the similarities and differences between Buddhism and the Bon religion.

As a kind of social and culture phenomenon of human beings, Tibetan Buddhism has exerted extensive and profound influence on the Tibetan race, gradually infiltrating Tibet's politics, economy, culture and other fields. What's more, it has also made its way into many minority nationalities. Groups such as the Mongolian, the Tu, Yugu, Naxi, Moinba and the Lhoba, are still pious Buddhist followers today. As a result, Tibetan Buddhism has proven to be one of the broad and influential religions in China as well as an important component of Chinese Buddhism.

Generally speaking, the role of Tibetan Buddhism was greatly weakened after the peaceful liberation of Tibet in 1951, especially after 1959, when Tibet carried out democratic reform, along with popularization of science and culture in Tibetan areas as well as abolishment of feudal serf system, which was characterized by the integration of politics and religion. But up to now, Tibetan Buddhism still maintains its broad and profound influence. Not only is it a social and cultural phenomenon, but also a significant component of

Tibetan traditional culture.

Besides Tibetan Buddhism and the Bon religion, relatively unknown to ordinary readers, there are still remnants of Islam and Catholicism in Tibet, both claiming a number of followers as well as sites of religious activities and active clergy.

A view of Zidru Monastery in Dinqin County. The largest of its kind in Tibet, the monastery has more disciples than other Bon religious monasteries in the eastern Tibetan areas. Its history can trace back to 2000-3000 years ago.

The Living Buddha Damzengwangzha of the Kurujam Monastery of the Bon religion in Ngari.

The Bon Religion

Strictly, the Bon religion is a kind of phenomenon of religious culture, as it retains an ancient form of this, and is richly characteristic of a specific territory and nationality. The reason is mainly attributed to the fact that the Qinghai-Tibet Plateau and its Tibetan nationality have never broken away from the prevalent atmosphere of religious culture since pre-historic society; that is, secular culture has been merged into religious culture, and there has never been a distinct dividing line between them.

According to archaeological excavations, as early as the Paleolithic Age, the forefathers of the Tibetan nationality have labored, lived, and multiplied in today's Qinghai-Tibet Plateau, known as the Roof of the World. The Tibetans followed the tradition of an ancient religion, which is closely related to their daily life, namely what was later called the "Bon religion". It is a prolonged historical course for the origination and development of the Bon religion, during which it established close relations with all aspects of Tibetan society, as well as the geographical environment. Therefore, apart from the situation of the prehistoric society of the Tibetans, it is difficult for us to grasp the historical origins of the Bon religion.

According to the ancient historic book *The History under Pillars*, the Tong, Tang,

Sei, Mo were four patriarchal clans that appeared earliest in the Land of Snows. They should be called the "Four Surnames" in a more correct sense, as until today there are also many Tibetans that continue to carry these four names. So, it is clear that the four clans or surnames are the origination of the Tibetan nationality.

After a prolonged age, the history of Tibet became clear: "Thereafter, (It) was ruled in succession by Seven Masang Brothers, 25 small principalities, 12 small principalities or 40 small principalities." From the frequent change of rulers and the social structure that kept dividing and reincorporating, we can learn the historical process and basic features of the prehistoric development of Tibet, as well understanding that it was a primitive society at that time.

When Tibetan society developed to a certain stage of civilization, the ideology of spirits and deities came into being, and there appeared many gods such as those of mountain, water, land, heaven and so on. As to the worship of spirits and deities, related Tibetan historical materials date it back to the late stage of the Primitive Society, but the detailed conditions are not available. Whatever, the ideology of the spirits and deities of the Tibetans gradually took form with the development of the ancient society. The view of "shamanism", or "animism", enabled the forefathers of the Tibetans to piously kneel down before various spirits and deities who were said to have magic powers. They presented all kinds of sacrificial offerings to express their worship, appreciation, or atonement, and they also prayed for good luck. *The History under Pillars* records: "Twelve talents, including Bonpo Sei, Bonpo Mar, Bonpo Tung, Bonpo Ao, offered sacrifices to the spirits and deities." This occurred in the 4th century BC. The twelve talents refer to the twelve Bonpos of the Bon religion. Here, the word "Bonpo" means "sorcerer" or "priest", and the words after "Bonpo" above are four surnames. It was from the "Bonpo" that what was later called the "Bon religion" emerged. According to many Tibetan historical records, the twelve Bonpos mentioned above were special features at that time, being both the priests

The Longevity Buddha worshipped in the Zidru Monastery.

in charge of all spiritual cultural activities and the tribal chief of 12 small principalities. Many countries in different ancient periods saw figures serving as both priests and kings, who were characterized as being half human beings and half deities. The phenomenon that those sorcerers served as kings, and at the same time those kings practiced sorcery is regarded as a general social and cultural phenomenon of a certain historical process.

As the Tibetan society developed furthered, about the 4th century BC, there emerged the first kingdom and its Tsampo (king) with a written record. It was an epochal change for Tibetan ancient society, as the old dispersed primitive society split up and a new united slave society began to emerge. Due to the basic change of social form, former sorcerers serving as kings at the same time gradually lost their power to rule. Thereafter, deprived of their positions as tribal chiefs, they sought refuge in sorcery, leading it to develop towards the features of a religion. This eventually led to the separation of religious power from political power. Probably at that time, the traditional religion of the Tibetans, the Bon religion began to take shape. Despite initial immaturity, after the supernatural exaggeration of the sorcerers, the Bon religion possessed its own extreme mythical religious rituals worshipped by the local people.

In a word, the Bon religion, originating in Tibetan ancient society and experiencing historical evolution and development, became a human religion with relatively mature scriptures as well as systematic teachings and rituals, compared with a natural religion which initially worshiped natural phenomena such as heaven, land, sun, moon, constellations, thunder and lightning, mountains and rivers and so on. The Bon religion underwent three stages in history, namely the periods of Dor-Bonism, Cha-Bonism and Jo-Bonism.

1.Dor-Bonism: The Ancient Bon Religion

In the period of Dor-Bonism, the religion began and slowly developmed. It was from about the 4th century BC, when Nyatri Tsampo, the first king in Tibetan history, reigned, to the 2nd century BC, and the reign of the eighth king Zhigum. This period was also what called in Tibetan historical books the period of "Seven Heavenly Kings". With regard to religious conditions, Tibetan scripture records: "At that time, the Bon religion had only magical powers to subdue demons and evils of the lower world, worship gods of the upper world, and pray for the prosperity for local people in the middle world. Something about the view of the Bon religion, however, hadn't yet appeared." It is known that the Bon religion at that time, with more primitive characteristics of sorcery, hadn't yet formed its theoretical system. As for the exact definition of its sorcery and its relationship to religion, it is difficult to come to a fixed conclusion from so many diverse views. Actually, in the early stage of history, primitive religion was mixed with sorcery, and it was difficult to distinguish one from the other. So some suggest sorcery was the forefather of religion.

The painting of Principal Deity Dalha of the Bon Religion, also in Tibetan known as Tangka Principal Deity Dalha of the Bon Religion, which is enshrined in the Zidru Monastery.

Generally speaking, in the period of Dor-Bonism, the Bon religion was characterized by its worship of deities and demons, which traced its origins to Shamanism or Animism. Ancient people took it for granted that natural phenomena were endowed with living and supernatural magic powers, so the initial stage of natural religion was called Shamanism. It was a religion that emphasized pantheism, featuring chaos mythology, and believed in magic powers. What's more, its sense of fear overrode other religious feelings. This kind of religious belief rose naturally from all kinds of factors that universally lay among the experiences of human beings, such as phenomena of death, sleep, dreams, illusory elements and so on. Through the process of simple logical thinking, a natural mental entity independent of the existence of the body came into being. In the process of the development of ideology, the mental entity was regarded as the essence of life, thus leading to the worship of souls, spirits and ghosts. All creatures in the earth have spirits, and these spirits were considered as the factor in the vitality and life that it endowed all things in the world. For instance, in the period of Dor-Bonism, Tibetans universally held the view that illness was caused by spirits and it was the spirits that controlled their fates. From these features of the Bon religion, it is clear that in the period of Dor-Bonism, the Bon religion belonged to the sphere of natural religions.

2.Cha-Bonism: The Yungdrung Bon Religion

The emblem Yungdrung (Nazi swastika which is the re-served Buddhist emblem) was introduced into Tibet along with Buddhism in the 7th century. The Yungdrung Bonism adopted this emblem as the sign of Bonism, and systemized the doctrines which included the way to pray for good fortune, medicine, victory in warfare, and how to arrange the proper funeral rituals, and the magic methods to tell true from false, and separate the guilty from the innocent. The period of Cha-Bonism, mainly known as the Yungdrung Bon religion, started from the reign of the eighth Tsampo Zhigum (in the

Kampos Soinam Jamei of the Zidru Monastery.

second century) to that of King Songtsan Gampo (in the 7th Century). It was an important stage when the Bon religion underwent qualitative change. The eighth king of the Tubo kingdom, Tsampo Zhigum, took several open measures to promote the development of the Bon religion. As one of his efforts, "Tsampo Zhigum invited three masters of the Bon religion respectively from Kashmir, Bolue, Zhangzhung to drive away evil spirits and had luck as well as practice other religious activities. Among them, one had the ability to ride on a drum to soar up to the sky to seek Terma (known as "concealed treasures", which means some treasured scriptures were buried by former masters in the hope they would be revealed for the benefit of future generations) by depending on his exorcising sorcery and other witchcrafts. He also performed his power to cut a piece of iron into two parts by using the feather of a bird. The second person was known for his power of fortune telling by using colored threads, oracle, fresh blood, and so on. The third person was adept at all kinds of funeral and death rituals." The quotation shows that Tsampo Zhigum introduced sorcery from neighboring areas to refresh or reform the outdated Bon religion. From then on, it began to emerge from its primitive and immature form into a new stage when superb practical magic was introduced.

The Living Buddha Zidru Dinqinerse of the Zidru Monastery, who was studying in 1998 at the Tibetan Department of Chinese Institute of Buddhist Studies.

According to *Historical Collection of Tibet and the Han*, when Tsampo Zhigum reigned over the country, the teachings of Shengyidorben of the Bon religion were introduced from Zhangzhung and Bolue of the western regions. After his son Pude Gungyal came to the throne, the teachings of Zonghetewo appeared, and there arose the Tanbonposhenpoche School of the Bon religion. It showed that during the period of Tsampo Zhigum, the Bon religion started its great change, beginning to form its theoretical system of religion and overcoming its previous lack of teachings and rituals. Obviously, the so-called theoretical system of religion was far from the "theoretical system' in the strict sense. In fact, it was only rough religious views or teachings and that it was called a "theoretical system' was only in

A Lama with the Zidru Monastery of Dinqin County showing a pair of bronze cymbals, an ancient relics introduced from the Han. Inside it is carved with a design of "two dragons playing with a pear" and words "built in the Xunade Age of the Ming Dynasty ", namely in the 15th century.

comparison with its previous form. Nonetheless, it was a great improvement. *History and Doctrines of Different Buddhist Sects* says: "Before the arrival of the three masters, the views that the Bon religion held could not be pointed out. After that, views and teachings of the Bon religion emerged. It was said that the Bon religion in the period of Cha-Bonism emerged from the Siva School." Here "the three masters" referred to the three masters of the Bon religion who were invited by Tsampo Zhigum from Kashmir, Bolue, Zhangzhung. And "the Siva School" is a kind of religious sect of India. Shitai'an pointed out in his book *Tibetan Civilization*: "Zhigungba, a famous Tibetan mythologist in the 12th century, said that when he referred to the period of Cha-Bonism, this was the starting point when philosophical system of the Bon religion came into being. He also embraces the view that the phenomenon was influenced by the teachings of the Siva School." Siva is one of principal gods of Brahmanism and Hinduism, representing the god of destruction, suffering and dance. *On Deva Nirvana* has it that the whole world was the body of Siva, and Siva, with two other gods, Brahma and Vishnu, indicated the creation, perseverance, and destruction of universe. So, sometimes, you can't find the statue of Siva to have been worshiped in some monasteries of the Siva School, and instead, it was replaced by a cow or the male genitalia as symbols of creation. *Records on Folklore in Tibet* also recounts the process: "Thereafter, Master Qingqoin, a famous scholar of the Bon religion, introduced into Tubo the theories of six philosophical sects in the period of Buddha Sakyamuni, and combined those theories with local Bon religion to form a new theory of the Bon religion, namely Cha-Bonism."

We can learn from this that, during the period of Cha-Bonism, the Bon religion, not only eliminated or threw away much outdated cultural dross from its formal contents and forms, but also managed to introduce or assimilate foreign religious culture from India that contributed to advancing the development of society. In other words, Cha-Bonism was formed by combining the ancient Bon religion, Dor-Bonism with introduced religious ideology. After prolonged assimilation, it turned out to be a new religion with theoretical content. Certainly, the close relationship between Dor-Bonism and Cha-Bonism cannot be overlooked as the latter was formed on the foundations of the former.

Here it deserves to be mentioned that a famous figure called Shenrab Miwo played a crucial role in the development of the Bon religion, and he was regarded as its patriarch. *New Red Annals* records: "At that time, Master Shenrab Miwo, who was born in Dashi, translated many scriptures of the Bon religion in the Zhangzhung area and made efforts to propagate it (the Bon religion)." Here "at that time" refers the period of Tsampo Pude Gungyal, the son of Tsampo Zhigum. *Mirror of Genealogy of Tibetan Kings* has a more detailed account:

During the period of Tsampo Pude Gungyal, the Yongdrongling School of the Bon religion had arrived in Tubo. Its patriarch was called Shenrab Miwo, born at Ermolhingren in Dashi. Many scriptures of the Bon religion, such as the Eight-Volume Kangqinbogyi and so on, were translated in Zhanzhung and prevailed in Tubo. The Bon religion can fall into nine sects, four sects in the Cause Bon Religion, and five sects in the Effect Bon Religion. The five sects of Effect Bon Religion discuss the ways to enter its highest stage, the Yongdrong Great Perfection. The four sects of Cause Bon Religion are Namshen Beitogyain Sect, Chishen Beicungyain Sect, Chashen Jushigyain Sect, and Dushen Cunchegyain Sect. The Namshen Beitogyain Sect was adept at calling for good fortune and increased prosperity as well as praying for the gods to cure the sick; the Chishen Beicungyain Sect engaged in death and funeral rituals, such as throwing funerary vessels and sacrificial offerings, performing rituals before the construction of one's house and tomb, and dispersing all disasters; the Chashen Jushigyain Sect usually practiced divination to tell good from evil, right from wrong; and the Dushen Cunchegyain Sect was involved in the rituals of exorcising evil spirits from the living, disciplining the corpse to prevent a ghost coming back to cause harm to the living, protecting a child from harm from ghosts, as well as practicing divination by astrology, capturing and driving off demons and ghosts. All sects used to shake rattle-drums as they practiced rituals.

The record above describes the principal content of the Yongdrong Bon Religion as well as how Shenrab Miwo, the patriarch of the Bon religion, built it up. However, as an important historical material, the record also contains errors. For instance, it points out that Master Shenra Miwo was born in Dashi, namely ancient Persia or today's Iran, which is groundless. If we analyze and deduce it from a scientific view, we will easily find that it lacks convincing historical foundation, although all historical books concerning the Bon religion stick to this view.

With regard to the doctrines of the Bon religion at that time, the famous Tibetan scholars Donggar Lobsang Chilai gave a brief account in his book *On Politico-religious System in Tibet*:" the new Bon religion was called Namshen, which denied the view of transmission of life and death, but it admitted the existence of gods and ghosts. It embraces the view that gods protect the life of human beings when they are alive, while ghosts not only control the life of human beings, but also can take their souls after death. So, people should worship gods who are protectors of human beings and drive off ghosts harming people." Until today, no historical works written by scholars of the Bon religion are available, and the histories of the Bon religion we read today are all written by scholars of Tibetan Buddhism or from Terma, concealed treasures. *Legend of Yeshechogye* recorded in detail religious rituals of the Bon religion: Every autumn there would be a religious ritual called "god sacrifices of the Bon religion", in which three thousand each of male yaks, sheep, goats and so on would be killed, along with one thousand each of female yaks, sheep, goat and so on. In spring there would be the sacrifice to dismember deer, in which four deer would be butchered with their four hoofs broken as a sacrifice. In summer there would be the sacrifice to commemorate their forefathers, in which wood and grain would be burned with the smoke rising to the sky. One should offer alms to redeem his life when he was sick, and the alms differed according to the economic conditions of the giver, from killing at most a thousand each of male and female animals to at least killing one male and female animal each. After one's death, animals also would be killed as sacrifice to capture or drive off any ghosts. In addition, there were other rituals such as calling for good fortune, dispersing evil spirits, divination, prediction and so on.

Lamas of the Zidru Monastery are pleasant and surprised at their own images on the screens of a video camera.

The religious rituals above show Cha-Bonism emphasized sacrificing animals to pray for the protection of gods and spirits. It seemed that all religious activities at that time would not have been held without sacrificing animals.

3.Jo-Bonism: The New Bon Religion

In Tibetans, the word "Jo" has many meanings such as "translation", "explanation", "compilation" and so on. So, Jo-Bonism refers to "translated Bonism" or "transformed Bonism". As a new Bon religion, it entered the third stage of its development. At that time, Tibetan Buddhism, its chief rival, had launched a large-scale movement to translate quite a number of Buddhist scriptures into Tibetan after overcoming opposition from followers of the Bon religion and taking root in Tibet. It was a new pressure to the Bon religion, already facing difficulties. However, the adherents of the Bon religion, who were not willing to fade away, tried their best to establish a theoretical basis for the Bon religion. They enthusiastically absorbed the lessons of history and reflected upon their shortcomings and defects, and then began to arrange or translate scriptures of the Bon religion following the example of Tibetan Buddhism. Hence, the Bon religion, known also as the New Bon religion, entered its third development period.

Tibetan historical record shows that, during the period of Trisong Detsan, some classics of the Bon religion had been arranged and compiled. The famous German Tibetologist Hoffman has conducted research to prove this fact: After the large-scale project of translating Buddhist scriptures was unveiled, the disciples of the Bon religion from Zhangzhung worked together with Buddhist scholars in the newly-built Samye Monastery. The most prominent translator of the Bon religion was Master Shangriwugyin, who translated the famous *Ten Million Dragon Sutra* into Tibetan. This is an important scripture of the Bon religion, retaining many contents and forms of the ancient Bon religion, such as the way to cure a patient and the legend of reincarnation after death and so on. With regard to the ques-

A follower of the Bon religion kowtowing to Mountain Zidru, the sacred mountain of the Bon religion.

tion when the book was written, there is no exact answer. But it is definite that it was from the period of King Trisong Detsan that disciples of the Bon religion made efforts to collect, arrange, compile and translate their scriptures and classics. Therefore, it is more appropriate to view the period of King Trisong Detsan as the formal start of the New Bon religion.

Monks of the Zidru Monastery of the Bon religion.

Many Tibetologists divide the time of the New Bon Religion into there different periods, and among of them, the famous Tibetan religious scholar Donggar Lobsang Chilai has the following account:

The time of the New Bon Religion can be divided into three periods. In the earlier stage, it was said that the Pundits of Lhuqoin had buried some records of witchcraft underground and he himself pretended to excavate those as treasures left by forefathers. Then, based on so-called concealed Tantras and some doctrines and rituals of the Bon religion, the New Bon religion came into being. In the middle stage, when King Trisong Detsan forced all followers of the Bon religion to convert to Tibetan Buddhism, a man called Gyiweijamqoi transformed some Buddhist classics into scriptures of the Bon religion. The story was that King Trisong Detsan sent him to learn Tibetan Buddhism under Master Renqencho, However, Gyiweijamqoi was unwilling to learn Buddhism, and in revenge collaborated with some disciples of the Bon religion and translated some Buddhist classics into scriptures for their use. When the king eventually discovered this action, he ordered that anyone who transformed without approval Buddhist scriptures into that used by the Bon religion would be killed without mercy. Many followers of the Bon religion involved in the act were put to death. So, Bon disciples were very frightened and, in order to ensure survival of their faith, they managed to conceal the unfinished works of

Gyiweijamqoi in a secret cave. These were later excavated as "concealed treasures" and handed down by disciples of the Bon religion. In the latter stage of the Bon religion, after the persecution of Tibetan Buddhism by King Lhang Darma, in Zamnyamtui there was a famous scholar called Shenkulhugyia, who tempered and transformed many Buddhist scriptures Bon ones. He gave them different titles and explanations in order to differentiate them from their Buddhist counterparts. They were buried under a great rock of Chowangzhewuqoi. The scholar then pretended to excavate them as hidden treasures buried by a former master. Following Shenku, many disciples of the Bon religion also converted many Buddhist Tantras and sutras to their own use. These also became known as the Effect Ways of the Bon Religion.

Available historical records state King Trisong Detsan at first adopted a tolerant policy toward the Bon religion. He created conditions for its spread in the same way as Tibetan Buddhism. For instance, he ordered the creation of special places where disciples of the Bon religion could translate or compile scriptures of the Bon religion and establish their own theoretical system. Actually, it was a cautious attitude the king adopted, learning from former kings. Once conditions were ripe to weaken the influence of the Bon religion, he would have staunchly imposed on it suppressive and hard measures with an aim of creating a broad space for further development of Tibetan Buddhism. In order to realize his desire to attain a dominant position of Tibetan Buddhism throughout Tubo, King Trisong Detsan, with great finesse, took the advice of ministers to hold a debate between the Bon religion and Tibetan Buddhism. At least, it seemed fair and reasonable, but the ability of debating on scriptures was a deadly weakness of disciples of the Bon religion, while monks of Tibetan Buddhism were highly skilled. It was obvious that the debate would end in defeat for the Bon

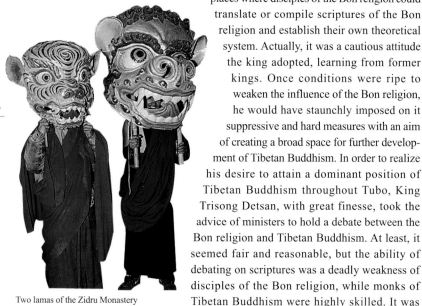

Two lamas of the Zidru Monastery showing the masks of Sorcerers' Dance.

religion. It was a hard blow from Tibetan Buddhism that the Bon religion suffered when their supporters were attempting to establish their theoretical system with full confidence. As the famous Tibetan scholar Donggar Lobsang Chilai wrote in his book *On Fusion of Politics and Religion* in Tibet:

As the two sides stuck to their own doctrines and teachings, the Tsampo sanctioned a debate between the Bon religion and Tibetan Buddhism and decreed that only the winner's doctrines would be permitted to continue to be promoted, while the side that loss would have to abandon their beliefs. In 759, a debate on religious doctrine between Buddhism and the Bon religion took place in Jangbu Yuan Palace, it Supo of the Meizo area, with the result that side advocating the Bon religion admitted defeat. The monks of the Bon religion were exiled to the remote places of Zhang Zhung in the Ngari area, their scriptures were assembled to be thrown into the water or buried under a black stupa of the Samye Monastery, and their religious rituals, such as the sacrificing of living animals to pray for good fortune for those living and dead, were banned. Only Buddhism was the standard. However, some rituals of the Bon religion, such as prayer for good fortune, dispersing evil forces, cremation, burning smoke to sacrifice to heaven and drive off demons, were retained but in an altered manner and became part of Tibetan Buddhism. In turn, the New Bon Religion that revived after the collapse of the Tubo kingdom, transformed and absorbed all doctrines of Tibetan Buddhism, and thus the Bon religion possessed its own doctrines and theories. It indicates that through continual and long struggles of the Bon religion and Tibetan Buddhism, in order to adapt the requirements of debate, both absorbed and assimilated something from the other by maintaining the form and altering the content. The Bon religion and Tibetan Buddhism both entered a new period of development.

Although King Trisong Detsan attempted to eradicate the Bon religion, he never took an extreme step to totally negate its influence. On the one hand, he decreed the abolishment of many primitive religious activities, such as sacrificing living animals and prohibiting followers of the Bon religion to tamper with scriptures of Tibetan Buddhism; on the other hand, in view of social requirements, he indirectly

Two women followers of the Bon religion paying homage to a mountain god. They walked around the mountain in a direction opposite to that of Tibetan Buddhist believers.

contributed to the maintenance and continuation of many religious rituals of the Bon religion. From the viewpoint of its adherents, during the period of King Trisong Detsan, the Bon religion indeed suffered the largest prosecution ever in the history. However, we cannot deny that, on the contrary, the actions taken against it actually advanced the further completeness of the doctrines and theories of the Bon religion. It is worth noting that the Bon religion not only survived through the continual suppression of Tibetan Buddhism, but also succeeded to enrich and complete its doctrines and teachings from Tibetan Buddhism. That is to say, the Bon religion had been greatly influenced by Tibetan Buddhism during the time when it formed its doctrines and theories. In terms of time, although the Bon religion began to form its doctrines and theories during the time of King Trisong Detsan, which is itself a good start, it was soon held back by the forces of Tibetan Buddhism. As the result, the final formation of the doctrines and theories of the Bon religion had to be delayed to the second period of dissemination of Tibetan Buddhism.

In the time of Jo-Bonism, the New Bon Religion not only matured in terms of doctrines and rituals, but also made great strides forward in religious theory. The greatest achievement in this period is that scholars of the Bon religion gave some comments on the religion they worshiped. For example, the famous "Nine Ways of the Bon Religion" divided the Bon religion into nine different stages as follows: Kashen, the way of Prediction, which describes astrology, ritual and prognostication; Namshen, the Way of the Visual World, which explains the psychophysical universe; Trushen, the Way of Illusion, which gives details of the rites for the dispersing adverse forces; Sishen, the Way of Existence, which explains funeral and death rituals; Genyi, the Way of a Lay Follower, which contains ten principles for wholesome activity; Argyia, the Way of a Monk, in which the monastic rules and regulations are laid out; Drangsong, the Way of Primordial Sound, which explains the integration of an exalted practitioner into the Mandala of highest enlightenment;

Yarshen, the Way of Primordial Shen, which explains the guidelines for seeking a true tantric master and the spiritual commitments binding a disciple to his tantric master; and, finally, the Way of Supreme Doctrine, which discusses the doctrine of great perfection. Among them, the first four are called the Four Cause Ways, the second four are known as the Four Effect Ways, and the last considered as the Highest Way. In fact, the Nine Ways of the Bon Religion classified a jumbled and numerous theoretical system and enriched the religious rituals and practices according to the tradition of cause first and effect second, as well as the sequence of religious practices. The theory of Nine Ways is as an important landmark achieved by the Bon religion, and was followed by disciples and adherents for generations.

The bronze statue of Zhabalhutun, the deity of Tantricism of the Bon religion, worshipped in the Zidru Monastery. It was cast some 1000 years ago.

4.The Development and Current Situation of the Bon Religion

The Bon religion, as an indigenous religion on the Qinghai-Tibet plateau, which had been handed down to this very day, has many famous monasteries apart from its long history. Now, let's give a brief account of the representative monasteries of the Bon religion in the second period of dissemination of Tibetan Buddhism and as well after it.

Tibetan historical records show that Zuqinnamkarqoinzong, the famous disciple of Master Shenqinlhugar of the Bon religion, built the Yarupenkharsa Monastery in 1072, and it became one of important places to practice the Bon religion. The monastery cultivated many

Mountain Zidru, the sacred mountain among monks of the Bon religion. It has been a tradition that younger lamas went around the mountain to worship the god of the mountain.

celebrated monks of the Bon religion. Unfortunately, in 1386, it was washed away by floods and was never restored.

The Gyikarishang Monastery was built in the 11th century by another disciple of Master Shenqinlhugar, Shuyarlhobo. It stressed mainly the practices of the Great Perfection of the Bon religion.

Paltunbeiqoi, one of close disciples of Master Shenqinlhugar, had contributed much to the development of the Tantric elements of the Bon religion. At first, he set up a simple place for practicing Tantric meditation, which gradually grew in influence and power.

In about the 11th century, an eminent monk called Meiwo Korparbeiqin established the famous Samri monastery, which is a hub monastery to study traditional philosophy of the Bon religion.

The four monasteries mentioned above, which also became the four kernel religious sites, are all located in the Xigaze area of the Tibet Autonomous Region. In terms of practice, Yarupenkhasa Monastery stressed scholasticism of the Bon religion, while Gyikarishang monastery and the Tantric foundation Master Paltunbeiqoi created placed more emphasis on the Heart Sutra and meditation. From the 14th century, the four religious sites went into decline. At present, apart from the Samri Monastery, which still stands thanks to several periods of renovation, the other three have been reduced to relics.

As already mentioned, the monasteries of the Bon religion built in the early stage of the second period of dissemination of Tibetan Buddhism eventually went into decline. But, from the 14th century, the wave of construction of the monasteries of the Bon religion revived. The first figure heralded in the new period was Master Nammei Xirab Gyaincain, who was a celebrated master of the Bon religion in the Gyialrung area of Sichuan Province and enjoyed high prestige. He went to the Xigaze from the Gyialrung area of Sichuan Province, and he tried his best to promote the Bon religion as he continued meditation. In 1405, he established the famous Menri Monastery, which is located in Namulhin

County of the Xigaze area. This not only holds a high position throughout the Tibetan areas, but is also viewed as the ancestral monastery of the Bon religion. It retains its influence today and countless believers worship there.

Another famous monastery was built by Dawa Gyaincain, an eminent monk born in 1796. He systematically studied the doctrines of the Bon religion from an early age and in 1834, he established a sub-monastery of the Menri Monastery in the Xigaze area, namely the famous Ralhayongzonglhin Monastery, also known as the Yongzonglhin Monastery. It was situated in Rela Village of Namlhin County, with the Yarlung Zangbo River flowing past it to the east. Up until today, as the largest monastery of the Bon religion in the Tibetan Autonomous Region, the Yongzonglhin Monastery houses over 60 resident monks, compared with nearly 500 resident monks in its heyday. The monastery enjoyed high prestige and has exerted great influence in the Tibetan areas since its foundation. For instance, the Kampos (Chief Abbot) of every monastery of the Bon religion in the Tibetan Autonomous Region as well as other Tibetan areas was appointed by Yongzonglhin Monastery. What's more, the monastery annually holds a large-scale religious activity to lecture on doctrines and practices, attracting thousands of disciples and followers.

Karna Monastery stands to west of Menri Monastery, forming with it and Yongzonglhin monastery 'The Three Monasteries of the Bon Religion', which compare well with The Three Monasteries in Lhasa of the Gelug Sect of Tibetan Buddhism. At present, the Nagou and Qamdo areas are second to the Xigaze area in terms of the distribution of the monasteries of the Bon religion. In addition, in Sichuan, Qinghai, Gansu and Yunnan provinces there are also quite a number of monasteries of the Bon religion, especially in the Gyiarung area of Sichuan Province, where the Bon religion has maintained strong influence. The famous Tibetan scholar Tukan Lobsamqoigyinyima states: "With regard to monasteries of the Bon religion, there were the Shendading and Yongzonglhating monasteries receptively in Tibet, and

Gyiarong Monastery. Later, the king took his troops into the areas and destroyed the monasteries and ordered the Yongzonglhadting Monastery to become the Gandain New Monastery of the Gelug Sect. He also issued a decree that the Bon religion was banned, but it was not strictly carried out so that, in today's Gyiarong and Cakar areas, there are still some monasteries of the Bon religion." Concerning the situation of the Bon religion in this period, Karmei Samtan Gyaincain conducted comprehensive and detail research leading to the following view:

Compared with the initial peaceful stage from 1017 to 1386, the Bon religion in this period suffered difficulties and hardships. When the Gelug Sect reigned over Tibet, in the period o f the 5th Dalai, the Bon religion and Gyonam Sect of Tibetan Buddhism suffered persecution several times. Many monasteries of the Bon religion, especially that in the Qoinbo area, were forced to convert to the Gelug Sect. In Beilhi of the Kamchu area, the most serious conflict broke out. Unfortunately, the rulers of Buddhism in Tibet, in order to conquer their rivals, sought help from Mongolian troops, driving all disciplines and followers of the Gyonam Sect of Tibetan Buddhism out of Tibet. However, the Bon religion, for unknown reasons, managed to avoid the devastating fate that befell the Gyonam Sect. Nonetheless, in the whole period of new theocracy, the persecution of the Bon religion continued. In such a situation, the Gyiarong area, as the foundation of the Bon religion for many years, succeeded in maintaining its influence by withstanding the invasion of the Qing Dynasty of Manchurians. In the end, Qianlong, the 4th emperor of the Qing Dynasty, had to turn for help to the Living Buddha Dranggyarobidorgyi, who owned supreme religious power throughout the Tibetan areas. In order to eradicate those indomitable followers of the Bon religion, Lama Zhanggya waited for an appropriate opportunity. In 1775, troops sent by Lama Dranggya set out for the Gyarong area and attempted to convert people's religious beliefs. Failing to achieve their objective, they demolished Yongzonglhating Monastery. They then built on the site a new monastery of the Gelug Sect of Tibetan Buddhism, known as Gandain Monastery. At the same time, Emperor Qianlong decreed that the practices of the Bon religion were banned.

It can be seen from the above record that, as an indigenous national religion of Tibetans, the Bon religion enjoyed profound mass foundation all over the Tibetan areas. The reason it failed to flourish like Tibetan Buddhism in the Tibetan areas is mainly attributed to the persecution it suffered since the 8th century. The ruling class of each generation, especially the theocratic rulers of Tibetan Buddhism, made every possible effort to suppress the Bon religion, so that it lacked the nurturing environment enjoyed by Tibetan Buddhism that its development required. Therefore, unlike numerous splendid monasteries of Tibetan Buddhism that are distributed over the central belt of Tibet, most of the monasteries of the Bon religion were built in remote mountainous areas. According to an investigation conducted by Mr. Phingcocheren, there are altogether 92 monasteries of the Bon religion throughout the Tibetan Autonomous Region, mostly in the Qamdo and Nagou areas (54 and 28 monasteries respectively), followed by the Xigaze area, with six monasteries. Lhasa and Ngari each has one monastery. At present in the Tibetan Autonomous Region, there are 3,291 monks, 93 living Buddhas and over 130,000 followers of the Bon religion.

It deserves mention that many doctrines and rituals of the Bon religion have evolved into the main component of the folk religion worshipped by Tibetans. In other words, many religious rituals and thoughts common among Tibetan folks can trace their origins to the Bon religion. Therefore, the Bon religion has exerted great influence throughout the Qinghai-Tibet Plateau, especially for Tibetan culture and customs.

A corner of the Potala Palace.

Tibetan Buddhism

1.The Origination of Tibetan Buddhism

Many Tibetan history books record that it was from the reign of the 27th king Lha Thotori Nyantsen (about 333 BC) that Buddhism was formally introduced into the Tubo Kingdom. But, according to Buddhist objects, sutras and small-scale statues that have been found and confirmed as dating from that period, Buddhist activities such as writing, translation, reciting and preaching had not yet appeared. With this, one cannot say that Buddhism was really introduced into Tibet as a practice. Actually, it was from the period of Songtsan Gambo that Buddhism began to enter the Tubo Kingdom. In the middle of the 7th Century, the Tubo Kingdom developed with an unprecedented speed, especially after the fifth Tsampo (King) succeeded to the throne. Seeing the kingdom was lagging far behind other countries, Tsampo Songstan Gambo adopted a series of open policies, introducing advanced knowledge related to science and culture from neighboring regions. Tibetan historical records show that Songtsan Gambo also had the Tibetan characters created. As a significant event in Tibetan history, many historical books recount this in detail. *The History on*

The bronze-gilded and life-sized statue of Sakyamuni at the age of twelve kept in Jokhang, which is brought by Princess Wencheng from Chang'an, the capital of China's Tang Dynasty.

The statue of Princess Wencheng worshiped in Yonbo Lhakang.

The Stupa left at the relic of the Guge Kingdom in the Ngari area.

Buddhism by Pudon says: "Recognizing the lack of their own script and literature in Tubo, Songtsan Gambo sent a group of young Tibetans to India to study foreign script and language; among them was the celebrated scholar Tonmi Sambhota. He studied grammar and composition in India for several years, then journeyed back Lhasa, and invented the Tibetan alphabet on the basis of one kind of Indian script. The alphabet he devised was composed of 33 consonants and four vowels, with the former originating from the sounds of the oral Tibetan language, while the latter were adapted from the Indian language. He also wrote eight grammar works." What's more, under the support of Songtsan Gambo, the Tubo king, the Tibetan script created by Tonmi Sambhota was ordered to be the standard throughout the country, hence it its introduction went smoothly from the start. Songtsan Gambo himself, by taking the lead in learning the newly created written language, soon became proficient in it, setting an example for its popularization. The invention of the Tibetan script, therefore, made it much easier for the introduction of advanced scientific and cultural knowledge and skills, leading Tibet into a new phase of civilization with the end of its non-literature history. It was from the 7th century, following the invention of the Tibetan script, that Buddhist Scriptures in Sanskrit started to be translated into Tibetan, which laid a foundation for Tibetan Buddhism to formally enter Tibet. *A Happy Feast of the Sages* describes the first translation of Buddhist scriptures in Tubo during the period of Songtsan Ganmbo, declaring: "During the reign of Songtsan Gambo, Acharya Kumara and Brahman Shankam from india, Darnu from Kashmir, Acharya Shilmaju from Nepal and a monk with the title of the Great Heavenly Peace from the Han were invited to the Tubo kingdom. Together with Translator Tonmi Sambhota, Assistant Translator Darna Goxag and Lhalung Dorjebe, they translated many famous Buddhist sutras and tantras in Sanskrit such as *Moon Lamp*, *Treasure Cloud*, *Mani Kabum*, as well as 21 sutras and tantras of Avalokitesvra, which exalts the virtues of Avalokitesvra (Boddhisattva of compassion). Through the translation of

21 sutras and tantras of Avalokitesvra, a crucial contribution was made, in terms of prophecy and imparting knowledge, to the dissemination of Buddhism in the Tubo kingdom. From then on, Avalokitesvra is considered as a Bodhisattva who liberated all sentient beings of Tubo from worldly sufferings, while the Red Hill of Lhasa, also known as the Potala, is regarded as the religious site of Buddhisattva of compassion, so that Lhasa became a sacred place.

The statue of Tsampos Sonstan Gampo of the Tobo Kingdom worshiped in Yombo Lhakang.

Meanwhile, some Buddhist offerings, most of which were statues of Buddha, were introduced into the Tubo kingdom. Among them were a statue of the eleven-faced Avalokitesvara from southern India, a life-sized statue of Aksobhya at the age of eight, by Princess Tritsun from Nepal, when she married Songtsan Gampo, a life-sized statue of Sakyamuni at the age of twelve, by Princess Wencheng from China's Tang Dynasty, when she entered Tubo as King Songtsan Gampo's bride. The last two not only were the most precious objects of Buddhism at that time in Tubo, but also symbolized the period when Buddhism formally began to spread in Tubo. Many historical books on Tibetan Buddhism clearly explained why the three statues of Buddha were introduced by the ruler of the Tubo kingdom with great reverence, one of which reads: "Three statues of Buddha respectively represent three different places, namely Tianzhu (India), Nepal, the Han, where Mahayana (one school of Indian Buddhism) prevails. In order to spread Mahayana in the Land of Snow, it is necessary to introduce the three treasures into the Tubo kingdom with great reverence." The record shows that in the view of the Tubo people at that time, Buddhism would flourish if they possessed the three statues. Consequently, the Tubo people, in order to house the three statues, spared no effort to undertake the large-scale building of Buddhist temples. *Red History* shows the historical process:" In the 69th year of Songtsan Gampo's reign, he sent Gar Tongtsan, a minister, to Amcuvarman, the king of Nepal, to seek a marriage with his daughter Princess Tritsun (Bhributi). The king agreed, and when the princess, reportedly the incarnation of the Angel Tara, traveled to Tubo, she brought with

Monks debating on Buddhist scriptures.

her a life-sized statue of Aksobhya at the age of eight, the statue of Sakyamuni, the statue of Candana Tara and other Buddhist statues. These statues were housed in a temple Songtsan Gampo built for Princess Tritsun, namely Jokhang. A second marriage was arranged with Princess Wencheng, daughter of Tang Taizong, and she brought a life-sized statue of Sakyamuni at the age of twelve as part of her dowry. This was installed in another temple Songtsan Gambo built for her, namely Ramoche. In addition, five statues of Avalokitesvara (Buddhisattva of compassion) were molded in the temple to be worshiped by local people. " Here we can learn that the first batch of statues of Buddha introduced into the Tubo kingdom were part of the dowries of Princess Tritsun from Nepal and Prince Wencheng from China's Tang Dynasty, when they came to Tubo as Songtsan Gampo's brides. Thereafter, the Tibetans did their utmost to build grand temples to house these rare statues of Buddha, pioneering the construction of Buddhist sites in the Tubo kingdom.

According to the *Historical Collection of Tibet and the Han* and other Tibetan historical records, during the reign of Songtsan Gampo, reportedly altogether 108 temples had been constructed; but available records show that only 18 temples can be located, among of which are Jokhang and Ramoche in Lhasa and the Chanzhub Temple in the Shannan area. The three famous temples were built to house statues of Buddha to be worshiped by the people, instead of accommodating a certain number of local or foreign monks, which was largely different from formal Buddhist monasteries in later days. So they were called temples rather than monasteries due to their small scale, lack of resident monks or large-scale religious rituals. Simply put, the first batch of Buddhist temples played an important role in promoting the dissemination and further development of Buddhism in Tubo. With regard to the three temples constructed during the reign of Songtsan Gampo, with an endless stream of worshipers until today, they are of crucial importance among the temples and monasteries of Tibetan Buddhism.

Songtsan Gambo laid a foundation for the practical introduction of Buddhism in Tibet by creating a Tibetan script and composition, translating Buddhist tantras and sutras from Sanskrit, and building temples of Buddha. But what deserves mention is that local monks of Tubo did not appear. Even the number of foreign monks invited from India, Nepal and the Han area were limited, and they were sent back after they finished the task of translation. A historical record supports the fact: "All the Pundits were satisfactorily rewarded after their translation tasks ended; then, they were ordered to return to their homeland." It indicates that, although the rulers of the Tubo kingdom had invited some foreign monks to translate Buddhist scriptures, they hadn't offered practical condition for those monks to live and spread Buddhism in Tubo. In addition, according to Tibetan historical books such as *A Happy Feast of the Sages*, *History under the Pillars* and so on, the following accounts can reflect the actual situation of Buddhist disciples in Tubo: During the reign of King Songtsan Gambo, two monks from western regions (likely to be from the Yutian area of the western regions), journeyed to the Tubo Kingdom, with an admiration for Songtsan Gambo, popularly considered as the incarnation of Avalokitesvara. Despite their initial wishes,

Followers of Tibetan Buddhism worshiping the sacred lake.

The Jokhang of Lhasa.

however, they had to return home soon after they reached Tubo. Since the public of Tubo had no knowledge of Buddhism and there were no monks, they were greatly surprised at the sight of two monks wearing yellow robes from western regions, while the latter were scared to see local people's customs and actions. At that time it was the Bon religion that dominated the ideology of the Tubo people, and consequently, what they said and did was in line with the basic principles and ideas of the Bon religion, which partly reflected the fact that Buddhism hadn't merged into the social life of the Tubo people. Even the spread of Buddhism had to draw support from the religious rituals of the Bon religion, thus limiting its own religious functions. An historical record of the spread of Buddhism suggests: "In order to satisfy the masses, (they) had to take the mode of the Bon religion and other related modes to lead the Tubo people to worship Buddhism; while, in order to protect the continuation of Buddhism, (they) had to bury some Buddhist items, including Buddhist scriptures, mantras, treasures and edict books, respectively under the four pillars, Mandala, and the Temple of the Dragon as well as other sacred places. "

It was a great open and reform period of Tubo society during the reign of King Songtsan Gampo. In fact, his emphasis appears to have been more on the reform of politics, the economy, military and cultural affairs than on promoting Buddhism. Therefore, in the period of Songtsan Gambo, Buddhism hadn't gained its foothold in the Tubo kingdom, and instead was accepted only as a part of introduced culture there. Whether or not King Songtsan Gambo was a pious Buddhist, he did support the dissemination of Buddhism in Tubo. However, as a part of his efforts, he did adopt some ethical percepts of Buddhism when he established the civil law of the Tubo Kingdom, as shown by historical records:

"Following Ten Virtues, (He) set up Sixteen Virtues of Morality which are of great importance to help Tibetans approach and understand Buddhism. The content is as follows: One should pay homage to the Triple gem; one should follow the dharma and practice it; one should repay the kindness of one's parents; one should respect knowledge; one should pay respect to the elders; one should be honest to friends and relatives; one should help one's neighbors; one should speak the truth and be modest; one should learn from decent people; one should be contented with the food and shelter available; one should not forget past benefactors; one should pay debts on time and not seek to reduce the amount; one should not envy others; one should not listen to evil advice but stand by one's own opinions; one should be polite in speech and avoid speaking nonsense; one should be patient and broadminded."

The establishment of the civil law seemed to show that not only did Songtsan Gampo have a general knowledge of Buddhism, but he also had a positive attitude toward it, with the result that he intentionally "introduced the content of Buddhism, Ten Virtues, into articles of regulations, and ordered his subjects to observe them." It was through the legal means that Songtsan Gampo introduced the Dharma and made his people accept it, contributing much to the spread of Buddhism in Tubo. In addition, some historical books have stated that, during the period of Songtsan Gampo, there were, in the Tubo kingdom, quite a number of people who practiced dhyana and samadhi (a kind of meditation). *The Blue Annals* says that "Songstan Gampo instructed many people to practice dhyana and samadhi, and a certain number of them grew to be masters." These so-called masters, however, were actually considered as hermits rather than

The outer view of Ramoche of Lhasa.

The Jokhang of Lhasa, built in the 7th century, has a history of over 1300 years old. It covers an area of 16,7000 square meters, with over 20 halls and more than 300 statues of Buddha.

Buddhist monks, for, at that time, there hadn't been any native Buddhist monks in Tubo according to Tibetan historical books.

In the ensuing period of King Gungsong Gungtsan, Mangsong Mangtsan and Dusong Mangtsan, Buddhism failed to spread further. On the contrary, a relationship between the royal court and Buddhism that had once been close gradually became weaker. It was not until the period of Tride Zhotsan that Buddhism once again caught the attention of the Tubo ruler. Here what deserves mention is that from the reign of King Songtsan Gampo to that of Tride Zhotsan, the Bon religion had been prevailing throughout Tibet, while Buddhism failed to take roots in the ideology of Tibetans -- although it gained transmission or continuation for a long time. Many Tibetan historical books record how Buddhism was promoted during the period of King Tride Zhotsan: "(He) sent Zengar Mole Gaxag and Nyizha Naguma to India for Dharma. They went to invite Master Pundit Formi and Forgyi when they heard on the way that the two masters were practicing meditation nearby. They were rejected by both, but they took back some Buddhist scriptures, such as *Agama Sutra*, *Suvarnaprab Hasattama Sutra*, *Action Sutra*, *Performance Sutra* and so on, which were arranged and presented to the King. In order to house these sutras, King Tride

Zhotsan built five temples, namely Kazha Temple in Lhasa, Zensang Temple in Zhama, Qenpo Temple in Nanre, Geru Temple in Zhama and Masagung Temple." The words above described the process of introducing Dharma and building temples during the period of Tride Zhotsan, another Tsampo with a positive attitude towards Buddhism after King Songtsan Gampo. It was he who requested marriage to Princess Jincheng, another princess of the Tang Dynasty. It seemed likely that King Tride Zhotsan's support for Buddhism came from his new bride, who was said to be a devout Buddhist. In 710 AD, Prince Jincheng reached the Tubo kingdom and was welcomed by King Tride Zhotsan and local people. She then began painstaking efforts to promote Buddhism, which had ceased its influence for many years. First, she moved the statue of Buddha, which Princess Wencheng brought to Tibet and had been buried underground for several dynasties, to the Jokhang Monastery. She arranged monks from the Han area to take charge of related religious activities in monasteries. In addition, she assisted Tsampo Tride Zhotsan to accept the monks fleeing from the western region and protected their religious beliefs:" At that time, the Han Princess (Jincheng), as a benefactor, invited monks fleeing from Khotan, Anxi, Sulo, Bolue and Kashmir, to the Tubo Kingdom, and built monasteries to house them for three to four years." The words above showed that Princess Jincheng played an important role in the promotion of Buddhism during the reign of King Tride Zhotsan. Due to her efforts, many temples were constructed and quite a number of foreign monks fleeing from western regions stayed together in Tubo. For instance, "(She) built many temples, such as Zensang Temple in the Zhama area, invited many foreign monks excluded by the western regions, as well as many Han monks from the central plains, to propagate Dharma. But the native monks of the Tubo race hadn't appeared." Actually, in a country lacking its native monks, it was not easy for the ruler to accept or house so many foreign monks, for it could easily spark discontent among ministers worshiping the Bon religion. So, when the new King Trisong

The rituals of turning Buddha.

Qamba around streets.

Unfolding Buddha Painting in the Zhaibung Monastery.

Detsan came to the throne after the death of Tride Zhotsan, all the foreign monks were expelled. *The Blue Annals* say that when Minister Marshang, an ardent follower of the Bon religion, ruled the country in place of the young king, he ordered all the foreign monks to be driven out of Tubo." During the earlier part of Trisong Detsan's reign, although he was an ardent supporter of Buddhism, he was greatly hampered by the hostility of the followers of the Bon religion, so many foreign monks were driven out of Tubo, taking with them many Buddhist scriptures. As a result, Buddhism was greatly suppressed in Tubo at that time. However, the influence that monks from the western regions and the Han had brought can't be ignored in view of their painstaking efforts, when they lived in Tubo.

In a word, Buddhism underwent a prolonged and complicated process when it entered Tubo. Apart from the events that Buddhist scriptures record and the objects brought into Tubo in the fourth century, it had been altogether one hundred years since the arrival of Buddhism, from the seventh century, the period of King Songtsan Gampo, to that of King Tride Zhotsan in the eighth century. During this period, the Bon religion had always dominated the ideology of local people, while Buddhism failed to take root and lacked the ability to challenge Bon, although it continuously attempted to exist or spread within Tubo society.

2.The formation of Tibetan Buddhism

As we have mentioned before, the first dissemination of Buddhism was spread over a hundred years, from the 7th century when King Songtsan Gampo reigned until the time King Tride Zhotsan ascended to the throne. But it failed to take root. Actually, the period was considered more appropriately as the time of a spread of Buddhist rather than of its formation. In a strict sense, it is from the 8th century when King Trisong Detson reigned that Buddhism truly began to gain a foothold.

1)The Achievements of Trisong Detsan

The Grand Prayer Ceremony held once every year.

Tibetans consider King Trisong Detsan (755-797), a devout Buddhist, as the incarnation of the Manjusri (Boddhisattva of Wisdom), one of the three religious kings in Tubo. The other two are King Songtsan Gampo, the incarnation of Avalokitesvara (Boddhisattva of Compassion), and King Ralpachan, the incarnation of Vajrapani (Boddhisattva of energy and power). King Trisong Detsan, together with the Abbot Santaraksita, and the Guru Padmasambhava, are regarded as the "Triad of the Abbot", who are always worshiped together in the monasteries devoted to Tibetan Buddhism. King Trisong Detsan was an ardent supporter of Buddhism, and during his reign, the religion started to gain its foothold in Tubo through his ceaseless efforts.

King Trisong Detsan, the son of Tride Zhotsan, was born in 742 AD, and succeeded to the throne in 755, at the age of 13. In 797, the king passed away at the age of 57 after a 53-year reign. In the earlier stage of his reign, the actual power of the country resided with Minister Marshang Zongbagyi, who was a supporter of the Bon religion and tried his best to hamper the spread of Buddhism. He was supported by some ministries and people hostile to Buddhism. Thus, King Trisong Detsan's desire to propagate Buddhism proved abortive. Donggar Lobsang Chilai, a famous Tibetan scholar, said in his book:

"At the beginning, King Trisong Detsan was so young that he couldn't rule the country by himself. So, Marshang Zongbagyi, an important minister from the former king's reign, handled state affairs. As a devout adherent of the Bon religion, Marshang Zongbagyi advocated that the doctrines of Buddhism were fallacious and could not be depended on, and only the Bon religion could be resorted to if one wanted to break away from persecution by demons and other evils. He also ordered that only the Bon religion was standard and any Buddhist followers would be deprived of their property and driven out to remote areas. Religious rituals after one's death were banned and the Buddha statues in Rampoche brought from the Han

A lama beating stone instrument to give correct time at the top of a temple.

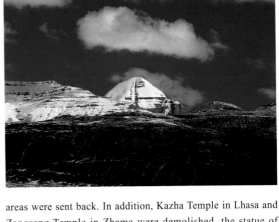

Mountain Ganrenpoqi of the Gandise Mountaions in the Ngari area, which is regarded as the sacred mountain among varies sects of Tibetan Buddhism.

The Mani stones wall.

areas were sent back. In addition, Kazha Temple in Lhasa and Zengsang Temple in Zhama were demolished, the statue of Aksobhya in Jokhang was buried underground as 200 hundred people failed to move it away. At the same time, the statues of Buddha housed in Jokhang and Rampoche were moved to Jizong in Ngari, and all the Han monks in Lhasa were driven away. They even hung the viscera from the slaughtered animals, and dried the wet skins on the scarified statues. "

The record above shows that at the time when King Trisong Detsan was young, a large-scale movement of suppressing Buddhism was launched under the leadership of Minister Marshang Zongbagyi, expelling foreign monks, prohibiting Buddhist activities, prosecuting Buddhist disciples, demolishing Buddha halls, desecrating statues of Buddha and so on. As a political movement seeking to restore the orthodox position of the Bon religion, it was a grave suppression of Buddhism just as it was trying to gain a foothold in Tubo, and it was also the most serious persecution it faced in a century. However, when King Trisong Detsan grew up and started to rule the country by himself, things changed in favor of Buddhism. At first, King Trisong Detsan sent Minister Sangxi to carry out Buddhist activities and take charge of the translation of Buddhist scriptures. But the work had to stop because of the obstruction by Bon ministers who supported Marshang. Minister Sangxi was sent to another remote place called Mangyu, in the Ngari area, to meet with another Buddhist minister called Basainan, who had already escaped there. Together, they made efforts to propagate Buddhism. After consultation with some ministers who favored Buddhism, the king succeeded in getting rid of Minister Marshang and his supporters, opening the way for the development of Buddhism. At the same time, Minister Basainan tried to seek Buddhist scriptures and masters, and when he reached India he encountered Santaraksita, the famous Indian master, who gave a direction on the development of Tibetan Buddhism. Santaraksita, also known as Boddhisattva Abbot, the son of king Zahor, was born in Bengal. He was ordained as a monk before the Master Treasury of Buddha-wisdom in Nalanda Monastery. In addition, Santaraksita, best known as the author of a great work of Buddhist philosophy called *Tattvasangraha*, was a famous master in the middle way school of Indian Buddhism. He and his disciple Kamalasia are representatives of the Yagacara tradition of the Middle Way School. The celebrated "Three Eastern Guru of the Middle Way School" referred to Abbot Santaraksita, his teacher Master Treasury of Buddha-wisdom, and his disciple Kamalasia. Because of his immense knowledge of Buddhism and his reputation in India, when Minister Basainan presented King Trisong Detson with his idea to invite Abbot Santaraksita to spread Buddhism in Tubo, the king agreed with pleasure. When Minister Basainan and Abbot Santaraksita reached Tubo, they were warmly welcomed by the king. But, unfortunately, Abbot Santaraksita's mission was not very successful. He spread Buddhism, gave lectures on the Ten Virtues and Twelve Introductory Buddhist Preaching in Tubo, but several months later, apparently an unprecedented natural disaster broke out throughout the country. The Pangtang Palace in Samye area was destroyed by flood, the palaces on the Red Hill of Lhasa were destroyed by thunder and lightening, crops were hit by hailstorms, and epidemics raged through the country. Most people, especially followers of the Bon religion, contended that these disasters were caused by the Bon deities penaliz-

The colorful Buddhist banners.

The ancient bronze conch, which is rare and only can be seen in the Sorcerers' Dance of the Sagya Monastery.

ing Santaraksita's Buddhist activities, so they demanded he stop his activities and leave the country immediately. Under the pressure of his subjects, King Trisong Detsan had no other way but to send Abbot Santaraksita back. Before his departure, Abbot Santaraksita advised the king to invite the great Indian Guru Padmasambhava, who could defeat the gods and demons of the Bon religion.

King Trisong Detsan accepted this advice, and sent two ministers, Sengo Lhalung and Deva Mecbuzhi to invite Guru Padmasambhava, who at that time lived in the cave of Yanglesho, Uddiyana. Legends show that Guru Padmasambhava subdued all kinds of demons and evil spirits on his way to Tubo, clearing away all the obstacles that threatened to halt the development of Buddhism. At first, when he entered Tubo, a fire dragon blocked his way by shooting out poisonous flame. With great ease, Guru Padmasambhava recited six-syllable mantras, turning fire dragon into a small lizard that quickly surrendered to him. Then, at Shampo, he encountered a white yak that brought down lightening and hail, with his nose steaming like gathering clouds, his roar like thunder, and his breath roaring like a blizzard. Guru Padmasambhava was poised to bind the yak with his lasso by reciting his secret mantra, so the yak had no choice but to pledge alliance to Guru Padmasambhava. Another time, an evil spirit was transformed into an old man wearing a hat made of monkey's skins, and used sorcery to make swords and arrows fall down like rain. Guru Padmasambhava transformed into the wrathful Vajradhara, turning these swords and arrows into flowers. Scared by the master's powerful magic, the evil spirit and his followers were bound and came under his command.

Because of his great spiritual strength and overwhelming power that the Bon magicians lacked, Guru Padmasambhava, the tantric adept, established the dominant position of Buddhism in Tubo it had been seeking for a hundred years. As a result of this victory, Guru Padmasambhava was able to overcome people's opposition so as to invite Abbot Santaraksita to return. Together, they planned steps to propagate Buddhism in Tubo.

Under the political and financial support of King Trisong Detsan, Abbot Santaraksita and Guru Padmasambhava made great efforts to disseminate Buddhism. Abbot Santaraksita mainly preached the Middle Way, Monastic Sutras, and other basic theories of Buddhism, while Master Padmasambhava showed his mysterious power to control the Bon demons. Tradition tells us that he subdued twelve demons of the Bon sect, and incorporated them into guardian deities of Buddhism. In addition, he imparted tantric teachings to the subjects of the Tubo kingdom. The most important thing is that he imparted to some young men and women whose parents were still alive, a mysterious magic called Round and Bright Magic, which was the first time that extraordinary abilities of the Secret School of Tibetan Buddhism were made known to the public. Donggar Lobsang Chilai, a famous Tibetan scholar, pointed out that the Magic of Round and Bright was the beginning of the magic of subduing demons in Tibetan Buddhism.

Tibetan Buddhism

Abbot Santaraksita and Guru Padmasambhava together contributed much to the construction of the first monastery in Tibet, the Samye Monastery. In 774 AD, King Trisong Detsan ordered the construction of the monastery under the direction of the two masters, and it was completed in 787. Someone believe it was built after the model of the famous Odantapuri Monastery in what is now the Indian state of Bihar, while others held the view that it mirrors the so-called structure of the imaginary world in Buddhism of the model of the Mandala of the Buddhist Tantric school. Each view has its supporting evidence. The triple-storied central temple represents Mount Sumeru, the mythical mountain at the center of the cosmos, symbolizing the center of the world. Around it are four temples facing four different directions representing the four continents in the world. To the right or left of each are two smaller temples, symbolizing the eight sub-continents. On each flank of the central temple stood two temples, representing the Sun and Moon. Four great stupas stood facing the four corners (south-east, south-west, north-west, and

The Phaba Monastery of Gyilhong County, constructed with Nepal style, is over 1000 years.

The Samye Monastery.

A piece of Fresco of the Zhaibung Monastery.

north-east, respectively) of the central temple. Four stupas of different styles, colored in red, white, black and green with different meaning (the white stupa stands for Bodhi Stupa, the red one for the Dharma Wheel Stupa, the black one for Serira Stupa, and the green one for Descension Stupa) to subdue various spirits and demons, and curb all natural and man-made disasters. All the buildings are circled by four enclosures in an elliptical shape, with four gates in the directions of east, west, south, and north, symbolizing a mountain near the border of the universe. The triple-storied central temples are combined with the Han, Tibetan and Indian architectural styles, with the bottom part in Tibetan styles, the middle part in Han styles, the upper part in Indian styles, while the statues of Buddha in each part of the temples are modeled after cultural characteristic of these three countries. In a word, the Samye Monastery was a mingling of ancient Tibetan culture, the civilization of the Central Plains and that of India. On the completion of the construction, Master Santaraksita and Padmasambhava presided over the unveiling ceremony.

It is known that the first batch of Buddhist monks was ordained in Samye Monastery. According to historical records, seven selected noble children were ordained as Buddhist monks by twelve bhiksus (senior monks) invited from Indian, with Padmasambhava serving as Kampos (president of the ordination ceremony). The event thus pioneered the ordained system of Tibetan Buddhism, followed by a rapidly growing of the number of local monks in Tubo.

Obviously, the successful completion of Samye Monastery created a new phase for the further development of Buddhism in Tubo. Not only was it the religious and cultural center of the kingdom, but also the special place for translating Buddhist scriptures from other languages into Tibetan. As a part of his effort, King Trisong Detson invited many Buddhist scholars and masters from the Han and Indian areas, together with local monks of the Samye Monastery, to engage in the work of translating Buddhist scriptures. As *Record of the Samye Monastery* described:

The translator monks are sitting with crossed legs on the ground, facing each other. One is reciting scriptures, another is translating it into Tibetan, the senior monk is correcting the translation; at last a younger one is writing on the paper with bamboo pens. At that time many monks, including "the first seven monks" in Tibet and many Indian Buddhist masters, Santaraksita, Parisuddhi, Vimalagarbha, together with many celebrated monks from the Han, Posang, Marhareza, Dewa, Mahayana, Harenabo and so on, assembled at Samye Monastery to participate in the work of translating foreign Buddhist scriptures into Tibetan. Besides Buddhist scriptures, the Han monks translated many Han works of medicine and mathematics. The directory of translated Buddhist scriptures is compiled and edited in the *Directory of Dengjia*, *Directory of Qingpu*, *Directory of Pangtang*, successively.

The word above was written according to the fresco of the translation hall of Samye Monastery. The walls on the corridors lie to the east, west and south of the translation hall and has pairs of frescos describing the scene when the monks are engaging in the translation work, which showed vividly the actual situation of that time. The frescos are of

The Samye Monastery of the Shannan area.

The Mani stones on the roadside of the Nyingchi area.

great importance to historical research on culture and religion, providing actual materials to people to understand and describe the past history. Quite a number of Tibetan historical books have the record that many great masters from India, the Han, together with local monks of Tibet, translated large quantity of important foreign Buddhist scriptures into Tibetan, such as *Monastic Sutra*, *Tripitaka*, *Tantra*s and so on. As a result, it is the largest ever scale of Buddhist translation since Buddhism was introduced into Tibet.

Generally speaking, during the reign of King Songtsan Gampo, Tibetan Buddhism underwent sweeping development under the powerful support of the King. For the first time, it had its grand and formal Buddhist monastery, the Samye Monastery, and local monks of Tubo, which laid a foundation for Tubo to have its Buddhist scriptures in Tibetan. Finally, Buddhism prevailed over the Bon religion and became firmly established in Tubo. But it should not be denied that the conflicts among different religious sections, especially between the Bon religion and Buddhism, were still fierce. Just as Tibetan famous scholar Donggar Lobsang Chilai wrote in his book *On Fusion of Politics and Religion in Tibet*: "The Buddhist ministers and masters from India and the Han insisted that Buddhism and the Bon religion can't co-exist, just like water and fire. It was ominous to

Lamas playing a tune of inviting gods and deities on the activities of Sorcerers' Dance in the Samye Monastery.

advocate the two religions, so only one of them could be permitted to continue. In order to decide which one should be supported, Buddhism or the Bon religion, a debate on religious doctrines should be held between the two sides. King Trisong Detsan sanctioned the debates and regulated that only the winner's teachings and doctrines were permitted to survive. In 759, a debate on religious doctrines between Buddhism and the Bon religion took place in Jangbu Yuan Palace at Supo in the Meizho area, with the result that the Bon religion admitted its failure. The monks of the Bon religion were exiled to the remote places of Zhang Zhung and Ngari, its scriptures were assembled to be thrown into the water or buried under a black stupa of Samye Monastery, and its religious rituals were banned. Only Buddhism was the standard." It was the third struggle between Buddhism and the Bon religion, ending with victory for Buddhism.

Another important event worthy of mention is that when Tibetan Buddhism started to hold sway and further expanded its influence, there were also competing groups that advocated different doctrines and practices among Buddhists. Two of the most prominent of these were factions representing two different traditions, the Indian and the Han, with the growing conflict becoming irreconcilable. Abbot Santaraksita and Master Kamalasila were masters of Indian Buddhism advocating traditional Indian Mahayana models, while the Chinese monk Mahayana, favored the approach of the Chang'an School. Abbot Santaraksita, the fifth disciple of Master Bhavaviveka, was the representative of the Middle Way School of Indian Mahayana, an orthodox approach of the Open School of Indian Buddhism. Abbot Santaraksita advocated following the Buddhist model of the five paths and ten levels, and argued that the process of enlightenment came gradually, not all at once. In order to follow the orthodox school of the Indian Mahayana, Abbot Santaraksita invited twelve bhiksus from India as his assistants to ordain the selected seven monks of Tubo. Hence, he enjoyed great prestige in Tubo due to his vital contribution to the establishment of Buddhism. It was he who suggested to invite

A Tibetan old man reciting Buddhist doctrines at home.

The Lamp Festival of Jokhang of Lhasa.

Guru Padmasambhava to Tubo; it was he who subjugated evil spirits and demons of the Bon religion, clearing the way for successful development of Buddhism; it was he who directed the construction work of Samye Monastery, creating a good environment for the propagation of Buddhism; and it was he who served in person as Kampos to ordain the selected seven monks of Tubo, heralding the monastic system of Tibetan Buddhism to guarantee the monastic institution. So, it was obvious that Santaraksita had many adherents in Tubo. When Master Santaraksita passed away, however, many monks invited from the Han, headed by Master Mahayana, preaching doctrines and practices of the Chang'an School, gaining many adherents in Tubo. Master Mahayana advocated a simple way of practicing Dharma, stating that enlightenment is attained suddenly and is not a result of gradual training. This kind of practice was popular with Tibetan Buddhist monks. It seemed like a tendency that the Buddhist theory of the Han had been prevailing over that of India. Certainly, it aroused resentment from Indian Buddhists, leading to a fierce debate between the two sides. Available historical books talk about the debate, and the most influential account is *History of Tibetan Buddhism by Pudon*, which reads: The King sat on the central seat, with the Kamalasia's supporters on the left and the Mahayana's supporters on the right. The king sent two wreaths to the two masters and asked them to pledge that the loser should present his wreath to the winner, and leave the Tubo kingdom. Mahayana is said to have began the debate by summarizing his position:

He who has no thoughts and inclinations at all can be fully delivered from Phenomenal Life. The absence of any thought, search, or investigation brings about the non-perception of the reality of separate entities. In such a manner one can attain (Buddhahood) at once, like (a Boddhisattva) who has attained the Ten Stages.

Kamalasila replied:

If one has no thought concerning any of the elements of existence and des not direct the mind upon him, this does not mean that one can cease to remember all that one has experienced and to think of it. If the mere absence of (consciousness and) recollection is regarded as sufficient, if follows that in a swoon or at the time of intoxication one comes to the state where there is no constructive thought. Without correct analysis there is no means of attaining liberation from constructive thought.

The words above show different doctrines and practices of the two sides. According to historical records, the Dharma debate was the largest in terms of grandeur and scale, with over a hundred followers of both sides attending. King Trisong Detsan presided over the debate. Before the debate, Master Mahayana studied profound theory and wrote treatises that denounced traditional dharma practice, and claimed enlightenment was gained by those in a sleep-like state. They also eschewed the practice of moral cultivation that Indian Buddhism insisted upon. However, the debate ended with the failure of the Chang'an School. The Buddhist materials of Dunhuang in the Chinese edition contradict Pudon's records and regard the Mahayana's sides as the winner. No matter; the debate was adjudicated by King Trisong Detsen, and he decided in favor of Master Kamalasila. Master Mahayana and his followers were sent off and the scriptures they followed were buried. Trisong Detsen further decreed that from then on Tibetan Buddhists should follow the Indian Buddhism mode and learn Vinaya, namely monastic disciplines. He also ordered that the fourth level of Tantras,

Sorcerers performing dance to invite statue of Guru Padmasambhava.

namely Highest Yogacara should be limited in translation, with the other three, Action, Performance, Yogacara, permitted. With regard to the question of which side was the winner, Professor Wang Sen has concluded after meticulous research: "the materials available today see continuous influence of the Zen School in Tubo, extending its influence to the Nyingma Sect and the Sagya Sect, while from records at that time, it seems that the Middle Way School of Indian Buddhism, headed by Master Kamalasial, was the main-stream of the religion people followed. So, it was the Indian monks who came to be supreme." After the debate between the Indian school and Chinese Chang'an School, although some monks of other schools were allowed to preach their own Buddhist theory, they had to adhere to main doctrines and practices of the Middle Way School of Indian Buddhism founded by Master Santaraksita , and his disciple, Kamalasila. As a result, during the first dissemination period of Tibetan Buddhism, it was the theory of the Middle Way School of Indian Buddhism created by Santaraksita that became the mainstream ideology in Tubo.

In a word, King Trisong Detsan exerted vital influence

in the establishment of Buddhism in Tubo, so he enjoys a high evaluation in the history of Tibet, and was immortalized as the incarnation of Boddhisattva Manjushri, one of three Dharma kings of Tubo. Following the demise of King Trisong Detsan, Mune Tsanpo, his son, came to the throne. Although his reign lasted only 21 months, King Mune Tsanpo strictly adopted the religious policy his father had established, making his contribution to further boosting the development of Buddhism. As a part of his efforts, King Mune Tsanpo decreed that Buddhist scriptures in the Samye Monastery should be worshiped regularly throughout the country, and Dharma gatherings for monastic disciplines and Buddhist sutras were also held regularly. He launched social reforms to narrow the gap between rich and the poor, and encouraged his subjects to donate to the Triple Jewels of Buddhism, with the aim of promoting a flourishing of both religion and politics. When King Mune Tsanpo passed away, Tride Sontsan, his brother, ascended the throne. The reign of King Tride Sontsan witnessed continual development of Buddhism: he ordered the renovation and reconstruction of temples and monasteries built by previous Tsampos; he

The Tolhin Monastery of the Ngari area.

Young lamas playing Buddhist conch.

50

unified the regulations of Buddhist translation by stipulating the translated Tibetan words; he constructed the Garqoin Dorje Yang Monastery; he built twelve preaching halls in Jokhang Monastery and Samye Monastery, along with twelve meditation halls in sacred places such as Yerba and Qingpo. After the death of King Tride Sontsan, Trisu Detsan, also known as Ralpachen, the third religious king of Tubo, succeeded to the throne, and pushed the development of Buddhism to its culmination by adopting several measures.

2). The Achievements of Ralpachen

King Trisu Detsan (815-841), popular known as Ralpachen, was said to have been the incarnation of Boddhisattva Vajrapani. The tradition of royal support for Buddhism reached its apogee during the reign of King Ralpachen. On the basis of the vigorous development of Buddhism created by previous kings, he did a great deal for the further propagations of Buddhism, leading it to the culmination of its development. Generally speaking, he made several moves in favor of the further development of Buddhism in Tubo.

First, he ordered a project to standardize the translation of Buddhist scriptures. The previous Buddhist scriptures were

A young nun in a nunnery of Lhasa.

translated in different languages of different countries, such as India, Han China, Nepal, the Western Region, Kyiashimilu and so on. Moreover, they were translated by different translators in different periods. So, to some degree, this obstructed the dissemination of Buddhism, especially to those who wanted to learn or were researching the Buddhist scriptures. As a result, King Trisu Detsan invited groups of foreign translators, mainly from India, with the help of local monks, to revise Buddhist scriptures translated before and answer some of the problems in their translation. Here it is worth noting that as early as the period of King Tride Sontsan, the work of revising translated Buddhist scriptures had been started. At that time, they first translated the Hinayanistic and Mahayanistic (different schools of Indian Buddhism) scriptures into Tibetan directly from the Sanskrit, then registered and wrote down the titles or terms to form an index, which was called *Terms Collection of Translation on Buddhist Scriptures*. Actually, it was a newly established glossary of Buddhist terms, also a bilingual dictionary of Tibetan and Sanskrit, to make the translation of Buddhist scriptures into Tibetan regular and uniform. According to Tibetan historical records, the translated language in Tibetan altogether was revised three times, with the last two done in the reign of King Trisu Detsan. Following *Terminology Collection of Translation on Buddhist Scriptures*, *Two Volumes of Explanation to Translation on Buddhist Scriptures* were edited and compiled, which was a large dictionary or theo-

The Medicine King on Mountain Medicine King of Lhasa.

Two followers of Tibetan Buddhism went past the Potala Palace on their way to turning Buddhist scriptures.

Followers of Tibetan Buddhism listening carefully as a lama lecturing Buddhist scriptures.

retical book for translation, with detailed vocabulary explanations and a large number of illustrative sentences. For instance, in Two Volumes of Explanation to Translation on Buddhist Scriptures, many difficult vocabularies and their explanations were listed in both languages, regulating the correct way of rendering. The dictionaries above are included in the Tripitaka. Due to their efforts, Tubo saw more a prosperous period in the translation of Buddhist scriptures. After regulating Buddhist terms, King Trisu Detsan issued a decree, which ordered that in no case were the rules of the translation to be violated, and translators were required to study the new rules to re-edit the scriptures translated before complying with the new terms. With the issue of terminology in Buddhist scriptures for translation and strict implementation, the translation of Buddhist scriptures was standardized. Most translated Buddhist scriptures complied in the Tripitaka in Tibetan, which were said to have been translated in the period of King Trisu Detsan, complied with the regulations of translation on Buddhist scriptures. Thereafter, the Buddhist scriptures revised under the new regulation were collected and compiled into a directory. During the reign of King Trisu Detsan, he ordered scholars to compile a directory of Buddhist scriptures, and in 824, the first directory of Buddhist scriptures came into being. It was called *Dangar Directory* after the name of Dangar Palace in Duitang, where the directory was compiled. Following *Dangar Directory*, *Qinpo Directory* and *Pongtang Directory* were complied, and the three directories later became the embryo and reference point for the compilation of *Tripitaka* in its Tibetan edition. Among them, *Pongtang Directory* was of crucial importance, because it was compiled in accordance with the classification of scriptures and doctrines, partly influencing the style of compilation of the Tripitaka in Tibetan edition. Unfortunately, *Qinpo Directory* and *Pongtang Directory* were lost in sequence and only *Dangar Directory* was handed down, becoming the main reference for the compilation of the *Tripitaka* in Tibetan edition.

The other major contribution that King Trisu Detsan

made to promote Buddhism was spending a large amount of money on the construction of temples and monasteries. It was said that he had built altogether 1,008 monasteries, among of them the famous nine-story monastery at Onchangduo, on the south bank of the Yichu River below Lhasa. It was built as a monastery and a palace. The construction style was unique and grand. According to *Song of the Cuckoo*, "the three stories of the bottom part were made of stones, the second three stories in the middle part were made of bricks, and the third three stories on the upper part were made of wood, with the whole style like a big bird flying to the sky. " The three stories of the upper part housed the statue of Tsampos, with monks preaching Buddhist doctrines on the corridor of the highest stories. On the three stories of the middle part lived resident monks, and the three stories of the bottom part was the living place of the king and his ministers.

Varieties of offerings showed on religious ceremony.

At the same time, Trisu Detsun granted royal incomes and privileges to the Buddhist monks. He decreed that Buddhist monks should regularly preach and recite Buddhist scriptures in the palace and in other monasteries, and every monk should be supported by seven households. If anyone dared to express his opposition to Buddhism or despised Buddhist monks, severe punishment would be imposed. The king even encouraged Buddhist monks to become involved in government affairs. For instance, Buddhist monk Ben

53

The 1000-Buddha Cliff of Mountain Medicine King of Lhasa.

The Buddhist banners at the foot of the sacred mountain.

Chanbobeigyiyongdain was an important minister in charge of religion, with domineering power over other ministers to interfere in internal and external political and military affairs. In order to improve the social status of Buddhist monks, King Trisu Detsun, in official ceremonies, would tie ribbons to his long braids, and Buddhist monks would sit on top of the ribbons, symbolizing his submission to Buddhism. Therefore, Dharma and Buddhist monks were given a courteous reception during the reign of Trisu Detsan, which inspired enthusiasm for Buddhism and furthered the cause of Dharma in Tubo. What deserves special mention is that it is from the period of Trisu Detsan that Buddhist monasteries started to be independent units in society, as they not only owned its monks and people as well as privileges, but also possessed land, farm and animals. It was clear that Buddhist monks had turned into a social class enjoying high position and prestige in Tubo at that time. Just as Tibetan famous scholar Donggar Lobsang Chilai said in his book *On the Politico-religious System in Tibet*: During the period of Trisu Detsun, he granted some monasteries land, farms and animals. From then on, some Buddhist monks began to transform into a landlord class with farmland under the management of their monasteries.

Thereupon, Trisu Detsan was considered an ardent Buddhist follower, and he was said to have been the incarnation of Boddhisattva Vajrapani. He devoted himself

A piece of fresco of the Potala Palace showing sorcerer's dancing.

to promoting Buddhism, worshiping the Triple Jewel, as well as ruling the country by observing Buddhism, with his subjects living a happy and well-off existence. However, his policy on Buddhism first, such as rendering high political privilege to Buddhist monks, providing financial support to the construction of monasteries and so on, spawned deep discontent among many ministers and subjects, eventually leading to the arranged assassination of Trisu Detsan, followed by a large-scale suppression of Buddhism in the region.

Generally speaking, during his reign, King Songtsan adopted an open policy in the fields of politics, economy, culture and so on. His reign also witnessed further intensified struggle and assimilation between the Bon religion, representing traditional culture, and Buddhism, symbols of introduced culture. Thereafter, Tibetan Buddhism, branded with obvious characteristics of the Bon religion, came into being.

3). King Lang Dharma's Persecution of Buddhism

King Trisu Detsan's fanaticism toward Buddhism aroused growing discontent of the ministers and subjects who advocated the Bon religion. In fact, some policies that the monarch adopted in favor of Buddhism harmed many ministers and political interests. For instance, he allotted a group of seven households for the support of each monk, which meant that even people who had little or no interest in Buddhism were required to finance its propagation. He also decreed that one should be punished by having the eyes gouged out for his staring angrily at monks, having the hands chopped off for pointing at monks with hostility, and be fined as much as eighty times the property value for stealing from monks and monasteries. The reaction against King Trisu Detsan's policy was so intense that some ministers gathered secretly and schemed to overthrow the current power and get rid of Buddhism. Their plot succeeded step by step. First, they killed Ben Chanbobeigyiyongdain, who was in charge of religious affairs and Buddhist monks. Then, they made a false charge

The clay sculpture of Bodhisattva holding a sword, also known as Chacha of Bodhisattva holding a sword.

A lama in a temple having his hair cut with solar-powered clippers.

A lama having his leather shoes polished.

against Tritsu Detsan's brother, Zangma, also a supporter of Buddhism, and had him murdered. In the end, Trisu Detsan himself was assassinated. He was succeeded by his elder brother, Lang Dharma, who was said to be bitterly opposed to Buddhism. Then, a large-scale persecution of Buddhism ensued. *Mirror of Genealogy of Tibetan Kings* describes the situation as following:

Thereafter, the territory of the kingdom dwindled gradually just as rivers in winter shrank; the Law of Ten Virtues was abandoned as a bundle of wheat falls apart because the straw rope binding the wheat has been cut off; the happiness and virtues of the Tibetan people disappeared just as the burned oil lamp; the strong royal government ended as a dispersed rainbow; the crime and street riots suddenly rose as sandstorms in a desert wantonly harassing all; the wish to do good deeds was lost as yesterday's dream. Buddhist translators and eminent monks had to leave monasteries and resume their secular life, leaving the translation of Buddhist scriptures unfinished. Those who were adherents of Buddhism had no choice but to renounce their beliefs.

The words above recount the events of suppressing Buddhism in the period of King Lang Dharma. Through analogy, it expressed a kind of sorrow and sympathy that later Buddhist followers had towards the disaster. With regard to Lang Dharma's persecution of Buddhism, many Tibetan historical books have varied accounts, so it was well known in every household in Tibet. It was a great disaster that Tibetan Buddhism suffered.

All the historical accounts have it that, during the reign of Lang Dharma, Buddhism suffered the severest persecution. In fact, the movement for suppressing Buddhism, with unprecedented scale, was plotted by some anti-Buddhism ministers, and ordered by Lang Dharma. In this movement, they not only banned all the orders of royal protection of Buddhist monks, but also removed all the prosperity and political privileges that monasteries and its monks had once enjoyed. Thereupon, the whole institution of Buddhism in Tubo was shattered. Buddhist monks were driven out of monasteries and forced to resume their secular lives, even ordered to either slaughter cows and sheep, or go hunting in the mountains. Those who refused were killed. Without any choice, many monks had to flee and live among the ordinary people, breaking away from religious activities such as preaching and reciting doctrines. The king also ordered the closure or dismantling of all the temples and monasteries painstakingly built by his predecessors. The destruction started from some famous monasteries, including Jokhang, Rampoche, and Samye Monastery. The statues of Buddha Adsibhya Vajra and Sakyamuni respectively in Jokhang and Rampoche were buried underground; others were either thrown into the water or smashed. They smashed down all the Buddhist objects in the temples and monasteries then concealed them with mud. Buddhist scriptures also suffered the same fate. Fortunately, local Buddhist followers concealed some Buddhist scriptures. From then on, Buddhism witnessed a dark period on the brink of extinction. It was a destructive attack on Buddhism, especially to the monastic institution in Tubo. At the same time, however, the persecution of Buddhism by Lang Dharma was an epochal event, as it brought to an end "the first period of dissemination of Buddhism", which was initiated by King Songtsan Gampo in the middle of the 7th century. That is, from the middle of the 7th century to that of the 9th century, Tubo saw its first

Women followers of Tibetan Buddhism turning Buddhist scriptures.

A Buddhist stupa of the Ngari area.

The Buddhist conch representing auspiciousness.

dissemination period of Tibetan Buddhism, which lasted over 200 years. And over 70 or 100 years after Lang Dharma's prosecution of Buddhism, Buddhism revived once again on the Land of Snows, which was called "the second dissemination period of Buddhism".

Following the prosecution of Buddhism by Lang Dharma, the political unification of Tubo Kingdom came to an end. Lang Dharma's policy to eradicate Buddhism largely hurt the religious compassion of those faithful to Dharma, and also aroused popular indignation, leading to another cruel event of assassination of Tsampos in Tubo. One day, Lhalung Palgye Dorje, a master who hid on the deep mountains to practice Tantras, saw a group of Buddhist monks being disrobed and forced to go hunting on the mountain, which made outraged and decide to kill Lang Dharma. In order to relieve those Buddhist monks from the king's persecution, he went down the mountain with his bow and arrows, seeking opportunities to assassinate Lang Dharma. According to Tibetan historical records, Lhalung Palgye Dorje shot Lang Dharma dead when he prostrated before the king who was reading the inscription on a tablet. As the king lay dying, Lhalung Palgye Dorje fled from the political center of Tubo and reached the Amdo area.

Lang Dharma's death led to the collapse of the Tubo kingdom and brought about a period of political chaos in Tibet. The royal family was divided into two sides, with two young princes supported by ministers on both sides. The ensuing fratricidal war was followed by peasants' uprising, which led to the collapse of Tubo kingdom. With no powerful authority in Tibet to hold the empire together, the Tubo Kingdom soon fragmented into a number of independent principalities. A new era of Tubo, namely the period of local authorities, emerged. Although Tubo entered the period called "one hundred dark years" of Buddhism, the flame of the Dharma hadn't been quelled. On the contrary, after the end of Tubo kingdom and the ensuing social upheaval, Buddhism received a better outward condition for its revival and development. For example, during the period of local

Buddha statues of the Tolhin Monastery of Ngari.

authority, Tibetan Buddhism shrugged off the central control of royal power, as well as the strict management of religious institutions. It made its way among the ordinary people and became a religion worshiped by everyone in accordance with one's personal desire. As a result, the prosecution of Buddhism initiated by Lang Dharma not only failed to completely destroy the foundations of Buddhism in Tubo but rather indirectly pushed Buddhism towards the ordinary people. The result showed that Buddhism had gained a large number of followers in Tubo and had exerted rather extensive influence among the people, due to which it could maintain its vitality, revive after destructive attack, and further develop in Tubo. Simply put, with the collapse of the Tibetan kingdom and the formation of local authority, Buddhism received an open and free space for its revival and further development, followed by "the second period of dissemination of Tibetan Buddhism. "

3.The Development of Buddhism

The development of Tibetan Buddhism, or its revival period, was regarded as "the second period of dissemination of Tibetan Buddhism". There have been many opinions concerning the exact time when it started, and it is difficult to draw a firm conclusion. Two comparatively identical views hold that Buddhism ceased developing in Tubo for about 70 or 100 years. That is to say, after a century from 841 AD, during which King Lang Dharma launched a movement to

Out of the Sutra Hall.

eradicate Buddhism, Tibetan Buddhism began its revival in the Land of Snows. In fact, despite the persecution of Buddhism by King Lang Dharma, Tibetan Buddhism hadn't disappeared in the Qinghai-Tibet Plateau; on the contrary, it still retained influence among the Tibetan people. Sungbar Yeshi, a prominent Buddhist monk of the Gelug sect in the 18th century said as follows:

During the period of three successors after King Lhangdama, namely from Nesung to Khore, In the Lhasa and Xigaze areas of Tibet, there hadn't seen any monastic disciplines, religious activities or rituals such as preaching doctrines, listening to Dharma, Buddhist initiation and so on. However, some doorkeepers of Buddhist temples or monasteries, wearing kasaya with collars, called themselves "Master Arhat". They practiced Buddhist doctrines, observed Buddhist commandments, and recited some part of the Buddhist scriptures for those died. Meanwhile, some part of the tantras (scriptures of the Open School of Tibetan Buddhism) were concealed when Buddhism suffered massive persecution, and those holding mantras (sorcery) or laymen practicing tantras handed down orally to their descendants or disciples. These tantras, only passed down orally from memory, were doomed to be quoted out of context and to be torn to pieces. So, as time passed, these tantras gradually deviated from their original content and were mixed with practices and doctrines of the Bon religion. In the end, those who insisted on practicing according to the misrepresented doctrines failed to grasp the true doctrines of Buddhist tantras and were confused about the stage of practice reached. Therefore, they only held a form of practice and followed various heretical ways of practice, leading to the decline or even disappearance of orthodox doctrines and practices of true Buddhist tantras.

Although most Buddhist doctrines and disciplines had been suspended after the persecution by King Lang Dharma, many so-called hermits or laymen still secretly continued Buddhist practices and activities, apart from their misunderstanding and deviated practices of Tantricism. At the same time, they tried to protect Buddhist monasteries, temples, scriptures and statues. Therefore, we should not deny their efforts towards the continuation of Tibetan Buddhism, which

A young nun enjoying pleasure with her nephew and niece. The Chamku Nunnery of Lhasa is accessible to any relatives of its nuns.

laid a foundation for its eventual revival. With regard to the time of "the second period of dissemination of Tibetan Buddhism", it is inappropriate to identify an exact moment, but we can definitely draw a conclusion that there were a series of landmarks for the start of "the second period of dissemination of Tibetan Buddhism". That is, In the tenth century throughout Tubo, quite a number of ordained Buddhist Bhiksu's (novice monks) appeared again, with the wave of resumed large-scale construction of Buddhist monasteries. As we know, King Lang Dharma's action to eliminate Buddhism mainly halted the continuation of imparting monastic disciplines, and once the regular ordainment ceremony for Buddhist monks were forced to halt, it was impossible to develop monastic groups. Consequently, if there was a lack of a cadre of Buddhist monks to play their key role, Buddhism was incapable of developing and flourishing. So it was from the 10th century when Buddhism started to revive through Tubo, along with the appearance of large numbers of ordained Bhiksu's and the construction of Buddhist monasteries. The revival of Buddhism was initiated from two main areas, the Amdo area, on the eastern side of the Qinghai-Tibet plateau, which was called "the lower route spreading Tibetan Buddhism", and the Ngari area, on the western side of Tibet, also known as "the upper route for the spread of Tibetan Buddhism". There then ensued the full renaissance of Tibetan Buddhism.

The 79-year-old Abbot Danzengsam of the Chamku Monastery, which is the oldest and largest-in-scale nunnery in Lhasa.

1). The Lower Route Spread of Tibetan Buddhism

During the reign of King Lang Dharma, Buddhism suffered its most destructive persecution ever since it was introduced into Tibet. At that time, three eminent monks, namely Mar Shakya Yeshi, Yogejung and Tsang Rabsel, holders of the monastic lineage of the Abbot Santaraksita, managed to escape to remote areas. They took with them important Buddhist scriptures and maintained the succession of Buddhist monastic disciplines, playing an important

A piece of fresco of the Chamzhub monastery.

Gongsam Gyaincain, from a well-off farmer family, had finished the study of a junior secondary school. Voluntarily, she came to the nunnery to become a nun ten years ago.

role in the continuation of Buddhism between the first and second dissemination periods. At that time, they were practicing meditation at the sacred meditation place of Qoiwori, when they caught sight of many Buddhist monks who were forced to go hunting in the mountain. Learning that Lang Dharma was suppressing Buddhism, they made a quick decision to flee out of the political areas controlled by him. Loading onto a young mule many important Buddhist monastic disciplines including *Vinaya*, they first fled to the western Ngari area. But they failed to take a shelter there, and traveled on to the place known as Garlo. Because of the obstacle of language, they had no way to spread Buddhism there, so they once again began their trek. In the end, by a roundabout route through Hoer, they reached the Amdo area (on the eastern side of the Qinghai-Tibet Plateau) and settled down. From then on, they lived and spread Buddhism at three places successively, first at the Crystal Grottos of Dando (at the boundary between Hualong and Xunhua counties of today's Qinghai Province), and then Diamond Rock and Arqoin Namtsong respectively (both in Jianzha county of today's Qinghai Province). These three places in Qinghai Province have been among the most important sacred places of Tibetan Buddhism, due to their contributions in sheltering the three Buddhist monks during hard times. According to *Mirror of Genealogy of Tibetan Kings*, following Mar

Shakya Yeshi, Yogejung and Tsang Rabsel, two other Buddhist monks, called Garwo Qoizhaba and Rondon Sengge Gyainsain, also fled from Qoiwori by taking with them the main Buddhist sutras and tantras, such as *Abhidharma Kosa Sastra*. In succession, the five eminent Buddhist monks unexpectedly met each other at Arqoin Namtsong, in eastern Amdo. Then, Lhalung Palgye Dorje, who murdered Lang Dharma, also reached Arqoin Namtsong, carrying with him some Buddhist monastic disciplines such as *Karma Sutra, Complete Vinaya of Vairocana* and so on. Unrelieved from his sin of murdering King Lang Dharma, Lhalung Palgye Dorje practiced meditation in one of secluded caves of Diamond Rock.

Due to the successive arrival of four eminent Buddhist monks from the center of Tibetan Buddhism, bringing with them the most important Buddhist scriptures, the eastern Amdo Tibetan area came to be the hub of Tibetan Buddhism at one time. Throughout Tibet at that time, no other place like the Amdo area can have had so many Buddhist monks and assembled so many important Buddhist scriptures. So, only the Amdo area met the basic requirements for ordaining Buddhist monks and developing monastic groups. Among the six eminent Buddhist monks gathering in Amdo, Mar Shakya Yeshi, Yogejung and Tsang Rabsel took the lead to cultivate monastic successors, that is to say, they succeeded in establishing a community of Buddhist monks who were qualified to ordain their successors. The celebrated monk Laqen Gomba Rabsai was ordained before them. Master Laqen Gomba Rabsai, called Mososeiba when he was born, was the nephew of Susei Sang, a famous local master of the Bon religion. At the age of 15, Laqen Gomba Rabsai encountered the three eminent Buddhist monks, namely Mar Shakya Yeshi, Yogejung and Tsang Rabsel, who came from the western Lhasa area, the center of Tibetan Buddhism. He admired them so much that he was eager to be a Buddhist monk and study under them. The three eminent Buddhist monks perceived that Mososeiba was a talented young man, so they told him he should experience a series of ordeals

The Khegya Monastery of the Ngari area.

The five-colored Buddhist banners on the roof of Tibetan houses.

64

The Diamond Thunderbolt of Guru Padmasambhava worshiped at Druba Lhakang of the Chamzhub Monastery.

before he could formally become a monk. Thereafter, They imparted basic Buddhist knowledge to Mososeiba and lent him the Viyana, sutra on Buddhist monastic disciplines. They required him to learn at first some knowledge on Buddhist monastic disciplines at home, and promised that they would accept and ordain him if he indeed was committed to Buddhism. As expected, Mososeiba showed strong piety after he read Viyana. It was said that tears flowed down his cheeks as he was reading, and his worship toward Dharma rose deep from his heart. When Mososeiba became a monk, he strictly followed the Buddhist commandments and studied carefully all the Buddhist scriptures. Five years later, he was qualified to be ordained as a Bhiksu (senior Buddhist monk). But, according to the regulation of Buddhist monastic disciplines, a new Bhiksu should be ordained by a group composed at least five old Bhiksu's, otherwise it was illegal. There are two different views in Tibetan historical books on how the five Buddhist monks held the ordainment ceremony for Mososeiba. The first holds that they invited two other monks called Gowang and Gyiban respectively to make up a group of five Bhiksu's. Although the eminent monk Lhalung Palgye Dorje also stayed at the Amdo area, he was not qualified to ordain new Bhiksu's, as he had contravened monastic disciplines for his murderous action. The second view agrees on the absence of Lhalung Palgye Dorje, but it insists that the other two monks were Garwo Qoizhaba and Rondon Sengge Gyaincain, instead of Gowang and Gyiban. Whoever held the ordainment ceremony for Mososeiba is not very important, for the fact is that, in the end, Mososeiba was fully ordained as a Buddhist monk. Thereafter, he studied with one teacher to another, and, at last, turned into a prominent monk with good command of the Buddhist scriptures and monastic disciplines. Master Mososeiba enjoyed high prestige throughout the Tibetan area in the early stage of the second dissemination period of Tibetan Buddhism, for which he was respectfully called Master Laqen Gomba Rabsai. According to *The Politico-Religious History of Amdo*, Master Laqen Gomba Rabsai was not limited to studying

Buddhism with his ordained teachers; he also traveled to the northern town of Yizhi to systematically study with Master Gorong Senggezha. The latter gave him four volumes on Buddhist monastic disciplines and told him:" I am a very old man, and I have not many years left to propagate Dharma. The hope and responsibility lie on your shoulders." Solemnly, Laqen Gomba Rabsai accepted the scriptures and promised to succeed in the cause of promoting Buddhism. When he returned, Laqen Gomba Rabsai went to Master Garwo Qoizhaba with whom he had studied for 12 years. *The Blue Annals* say that Master Laqen Gomba Rabsai was famous for the depth of his Buddhist knowledge and ethical virtues among the local people throughout the Amdo area. What's more, he gradually exerted an important influence in disseminating Buddhism. Master Laqen Gomba Rabsai made Dando the center of his Buddhist cause, holding various Buddhist actives such as worshiping the Triple Jewels, sacrificing to the guardian deities of Dharma and so on. He also prayed to the local gods to aid him in propagating Buddhism. His flock of Buddhist adherents grew remarkably. Under the sponsorship of the local power, he embarked on the construction of monasteries, stupas and other Buddhist buildings in Dando. The famous Dando Monastery thus came into being. Master Laqen Gomba Rabsai reached the spot at the age of 49 and remained until he attained Nirvana at the age of 84. Due to his rising reputation, many Buddhist followers were attracted to Dando Monastery and requested to be ordained before him. According to Tibetan historical books, Bargoyesheyongzong, Paneidamzhabao, also called Monk Ba and Pa in historical works, were the first two monks ordained as Bhiksu's before him, followed by eight others. Baguo Yeshe Yongzong succeeded him and ordained his disciple Zheng Yeshe Gyaincain as a Buddhist monk.

As we know, Master Laqen Gomba Rabsai spread the monastic disciplines of Buddhism in eastern Amdo, making every possible effort to cultivate Buddhist Bhiksu's and advocate Tibetan Buddhism. When his achievements spread to the Lhasa area, where Tibetan Buddhism originated,

A piece of fresco of the Potala Palace showing the Butter Lamp Festival.

A piece of fresco of the Dalai Summer Palace Lhobolhinka showing that Sakyamuni is lecturing Buddhist scriptures.

The Great Mighty Holy Diamond Mandala kept in the Palace Museum of Beijing.

immediately, local feudal lords actively responded. At that time, according to *Historical Records of Tibet and the Han*, the Lhasa area was ruled by descendents of Yundein, one of sons of King Lhangdama. Yundein and the Imperial Concubine Bacho Zhaxichu, who had given birth to a boy called Tride Gungnyen, who, turn, had two sons, Tride Rigargung and Tride Nyimagun. Tride Nyingmagun's son was called Tride Nyiwogung, and his descendents lived around Lhungshe, Pengyu, Amdo and Kamqo. Tride Ribargung had two sons called Tride Bo and Dorgyiba, and the former had two sons called Wubargyi and Tanglhazhaba, while the latter's son was called Chiwang Qoicain. Chana Yeshe Gyaincain, the son of Chiwang Qoicain, was the lord of Samye in the Lhasa area, and he was also a famous person in the history of Tibetan Buddhism, having supported its revival in the second period of dissemination. *Red Annals* states the following:

When Yeshe Gyaincain, the lord of Samye in the Lhasa area, heard that the Buddhist monastic lineage was reviving in the Amdo area, he showed so great enthusiasm and immediately sent his Buddhist disciples to receive ordination and also introduced the lineage of Buddhist monastic disciplines. Altogether, ten Buddhist disciples, five from the Lhasa area and the other five from the Xigaze area, reached Dando Monastery in succession to receive ordination. They were: Lhumei Cechen Xirab, Zhang Yeshe Yongden, Reshe Cecheng

Joinnei, Bar Cecheng Lobzui, Sungba Yeshe Lobzui (the five Buddhist monks from the Lhasa area), Lodon Dorje Wangshiu, Congzeng Xirab Senge, Brothers Ahli Baraogyi, Pudongpawopadigar (from the Xigaze area).

The lineage of Yundain's Descendants
These ten Buddhist monks were ordained in Dando

The Rito Monastery of the Ngari area.

Monastery before Master Zheng Yeshe Gyaincain, one of close disciples of Master Laqen Gomba Rabsai in lineal succession. Once ordained, the new Bhiksu's went back and continued to propagate Buddhism respectively in the Lhasa and Xigaze areas, building monasteries and enlarging the number of monks. With regard to the accounts of the Buddhist disciples from the Lhasa and Xigaze areas who went to Dando monastery, especially regarding the lineage of teachers and disciples as well as the number of ordained disciples, different accounts have appeared in Tibetan historical works: History on Buddhism by Purdain records that the ten Buddhist disciples went to Dando Monastery to receive ordination, while *The Mirror of Genealogy of Tibetan Kings* states that altogether 12 Buddhist disciples in succession received Buddhist ordination and succeeded in the lineage of Buddhist monastic disciplines, with a group of seven reaching Dando Monastery first, followed by the other five.

Whether there were ten or twelve disciples, all of them, especially the five from the Lhasa area, made great contributions to the revival of Tibetan Buddhism in its second period of dissemination. When the five returned to the Lhasa

67

The Buddha's niche in a household of Lhasa.

Lamas of the Zhaibung Monastery of Lhasa watch TV through satellite television receiver housed on the roof, and hot water are easily available by using solar cooking utensils.

68

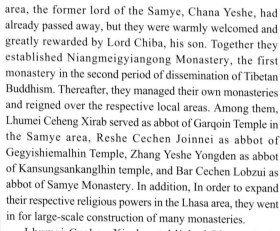

The clay sculpture of Buddha, also known as Buddha Chacha, which is housed in the Songzong Monastery of Bomi County of the Tibetan Autonomous Region.

area, the former lord of the Samye, Chana Yeshe, had already passed away, but they were warmly welcomed and greatly rewarded by Lord Chiba, his son. Together they established Niangmeigyiangong Monastery, the first monastery in the second period of dissemination of Tibetan Buddhism. Thereafter, they managed their own monasteries and reigned over the respective local areas. Among them, Lhumei Ceheng Xirab served as abbot of Garqoin Temple in the Samye area, Reshe Cechen Joinnei as abbot of Gegyishiemalhin Temple, Zhang Yeshe Yongden as abbot of Kansungsankanglhin temple, and Bar Cechen Lobzui as abbot of Samye Monastery. In addition, In order to expand their respective religious powers in the Lhasa area, they went in for large-scale construction of many monasteries.

Lhumei Cechen Xirab established Lhamuchedu Monastery as his base to promote Buddhism, and his four close disciples went on to form their respective schools belonging to the Lhumei School. Among of them, Zhumeicechenjoinnei built Soimetanqin Monastery as his base and established the Tang Branch; Shangneinamdowangshiu established the Shang Branch, with the Recha and Gyi monasteries as his base; Dorjamqoijoinna created the Dor Branch, with Yepapare Monastery as his base; and Lanyeshexirab created the Lan Branch, with Gyiagang Monastery as his base.

Four Branches of Lhumel School In the Lhasa area

Tang Branch	Foundations	Founders
Shang Branch	Soimetanqin Monastery	Zhumeicechenjoinnei
Dor Branch	Recha and Gyi Monasteries	Shangneinamdowangshiu
YepapaRe Monastery	YepapaRe Monastery	Dorjamqoijoinna
Lan Branch	Gyiagang Monastery	Lanyeshexirab

Besides the Lhumei School, there were also others. Sungba Yeshe Lobzui constructed Chamei Monastery in Chosa, but his influence soon declined and gradually disappeared; Reshe Cechen Joinnei built Changbwo Monastery in Mozhu and created the Re School; Bar Cechen Lobzui created the Bar School with its base at Nambargyibo Monastery in Pengbo; Zhang Yeshe Jongdam established the Zhang School by constructing Ennamgyimo Monastery as his base.

Four Schools in Lhasa area of Lower Route Spread of Buddhism

Schools	Foundations	Founders
Lhumel	Lhamuchedu Monastery	Lhumei Cenhen Xirab
Re School	Changbwo Monasteries	Reshe Cechen Joinne
Bar School	Nambargyibo Monastery	Bar Cechen Lobzui
Zhang School	Ennamgyimo Monastery	Zhang Yeshe Jongdam

The turning Buddhist wheel on sale before Jokhang of Lhasa.

The five Buddhist disciples from Lhasa who went to the Amdo area and were ordained before Laqen Gomba Rabsai, except Sungba Yeshe Lobzui, all created their own schools with chief monasteries as their base. They competed to expand their religious powers in the Lhasa area, eventually leading to continuous conflict. The famous Tibetan scholar Donggar Lobsang Chilai says in his book:

In 1106, the Lhumei School fought a war with the Bar and Re schools. Many temples around the Samye Monastery were burnt down, and the enclosures around the Samye also collapsed. Translator Re Dorgyizha organized the work of reconstruction of these monasteries. At that time, large amounts of wood were carried from Aokar, and over 500 craftsmen and workers were recruited to

The colorful Buddhist banners on the bank of Lhasa River.

An artisan renovating the fresco of the Chamzhub Monastery.

reconstruct and renovate Samye Monastery. It took over two years and consumed more that 100,000 dous of grain to finish the reconstruction. Recherab, the disciple of Translator Re, has described the event in detail in his book Biography of Translator Re Dorgyezha. In 1160, another fight broke out among the four schools in Lhasa, Yalhung, Pengbo and so on. Many monasteries in Lhasa, including Jokhang, Ramoche, and Changzhub Monastery were badly damaged. At that time, Dargung Cechen Nyingbo, the disciple of Tabo Lhagye, came out to resolve the conflict by meditation. He ordered the renovation of Jokhang and Ramoche in the Lhasa area, and placed the two temples under the command of Gongtanglamajang, the founder of the Caiba Branch of the Garge Sect who at that time had the most influential political and military power in the Lhasa area.

The four schools of Lhumei Cechen Xirab, Bar Cechen Lobzui, Reshe Cechen Joinne, Zhang Yeshe Jongdam in the Lhasa area, although belonging to one sect, sought to expand their respective powers in politics, religion and the economy by engaging in continuous wars over a lengthy period. Their conflicts cast a shadow over Tibetan Buddhism in the Lhasa area.

Simply put, in the second period of dissemination of Tibetan Buddhism, many eminent scholars and monks, or important political figures, such as Master Laqen Gomba Rabsai and his successors, the ten disciples in the Lhasa and Xigaze areas who were ordained by Master Laqen Gomba Rabsai, especially Lhumei Cechen Xirab, and the lord of the Samye Chana Yeshe Gyaincain, had been of great importance to the revival and further promotion of Tibetan Buddhism, enjoying high prestige as a result.

2). The Upper Route Spread of Tibetan Buddhism

A single spark of Tibetan Buddhism from the Dando Monastery soon turned into a prairie fire throughout the Amdo Tibetan area. The revival of Tibetan Buddhism first started from the lower route of the Amdo area, which is also known as "the lower route spread of Tibetan Buddhism", which marked the history of Tibetan Buddhism during the opening of the second period of dissemination. At the same time, in the western areas of the Tibet Autonomous Region, the Ngari area also launched a Buddhism revival movement. As it appeared on the upper route of the Ngari area, Tibetologists called it the "the upper route spread of Tibetan Buddhism".

After King Lhang Darma was killed, his two sons, Yundain and Wosung, fought each other for a lengthy period. Their war also brought on a period of political chaos in Tibet. In the end, Wosung was defeated in the Lhasa area and fled to Ngari, where he set up new base. It was said that Paikhecain, the son of Wosung, reconstructed and renovated the Nyingmei and Chopomeilhung monasteries and six others. Paikhecain had two sons, Gyide Nyimagung and Chiza Shizebeipai. At that time, the forces of Gyide Nyimagung and Chiza Shizebeipai were driven out of the Lhasa area by the descendants' of Yundain: Chiza Shizebeipai retreated to Lhachei and left no records; while Gyide Nyimagung fled to Ngari, built political power there and made efforts to expand his strength. Gyide Nyimagung had three sons, Paigyigung, Tezugung, Zhaxigung. They were also were known as the Three kings of Ngari Region, each of whom controlled certain areas that became the "Three areas of Ngari" in Tibetan geography. The oldest son

Eminent monks performing religious rituals.

The Palkor Monastery of Gyangze County.

Paigyigung ruled over the Mangyu area, namely today's Lhadake area, and later built the lineage of King Lhadake; the second son Tezugung controlled the Burang area; the youngest son Zhaxigung controlled the Zhangzhung area, today's Ngari area, and later built the Guge Kingdom. Zhaxigung had two sons, Khore and Sungbei, and the former also had two sons, Nagarozha and Tewarozha. Khore was the famous Lha lama Yesho O in the history of Tibetan Buddhism. In his old age (near the end of tenth century), Khore's deep love and reverence toward Buddhism was so strong that he preferred to renounce the throne and become a Buddhist monk to promote the cause of Dharma. Following ancestral tradition, He delivered the throne to his little brother, Sungbei, and vowed to be a Buddhist monk before a statue of Buddha, taking the ordination name Lha lama Yeshe O. Thereafter, his two sons, Nagar Rezha and Dewa Rezha also followed him and became Buddhist monks. Lha Lama Yeshe O was the first person to promote Buddhism in the Ngari area, and he also contributed much to the revival of Tibetan Buddhism. So Lha lama Yeshe O, respectfully regarded as the founder of "the upper route spread of Tibetan Buddhism", together with Laqen Gombar Rabsai, who pioneered the revival of Buddhism in Amdo, were recorded in Tibetan historical works.

Lamas debating on Buddhist scriptures.

The Lineage of Wosung's Descendants

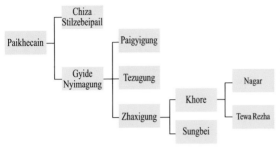

The paintings of Auspicious Tara.

Mirroring the Samye Monastery of the Lhasa area, Lha Lama Yeshe O built the Totan Paigyi Lhakang, later called Tolin Monastery, which was located at Zhasung of Zhada county in the Ngari area. It was the first monastery to be built in the Ngari area after the persecution of Buddhism by Lhang Dharma, and it was also the dominant site for the propagation of Buddhism at this time. This was in itself a great achievement, but it was not enough for Lha Lama Yeshe O. He sent 21 promising Tibetan noble monks, together with fourteen servants, to Kashmir to study, as Buddhism was flourishing there. All but two of the monks died of illness or from heat exhaustion, but the two who returned became prominent scholars and translators. They were Reqen Sampo and Lekbe Sherap, who were respectfully called the No.1 translator and the No.2 translator.

Translator Renqin Sampo was born in the Ngari area and was ordained as a monk by Master Kampos Yeshe Sampo. When he was young, he went to Kashmir several times and followed many celebrated masters to study sutras and tantras. Translator Renqen Sampos recorded great achievements in Buddhist scriptures, becoming a shining pearl in the field of Tibetan Buddhism at that time. Lha Detsan, the king of the Ngari area, not only honored him as the first man to be worshiped, but also acknowledged him as the monarch's Vajra master. Furthermore, In order to recog-

The Guardian Deities of Gombo in the Guardian Deities' Dance in winter of the Sagya Monastery.

The 1000-Buddha fresco of the Zhatam Monastery of Zhanam County of the Tibetan Autonomous Region. The fresco, permeating with an Indian style, was painted in 1081 when the monastery was built.

Eminent monks of the Grand Prayer Ceremony.

nize Renqin Sampo's great achievements, King Lha Detsan placed several areas under his control to become a base for religious activities and where the king built a number of temples and stupas for his master. Under the patronage of King Lha Detsan, Translator Renqen Sampo, presided over the construction of many temples and stupas, such as the Chaza Temple, the Rongdi Temple and so on.

The greatest contribution of Renqen Sampo, however, lay in the way he devoted himself to translating Buddhist scriptures. He translated many Sanskrit sutras and tantras, the latter being regarded as marking the inauguration of neo-secret Buddhist scriptures. Altogether 17 sutras, 33 commentaries on Buddhist scriptures and 108 tantras were translated. Some important tantras, such as *Collection of Tantras*, *Tantras on Reality*, and *Explanation of Ananda Tantra* were among them. In addition, some Buddhist scriptures previously translated were revised under the direction of Translator Renqin Sampo, helping to create a new edition of Sanskrit scriptures. It was from the time of Renqin Sampo that the translation of Buddhist tantras was divided into two periods. Before his time were the old tantras, mainly translated by masters of the Tubo Kingdom, while from time there were the new tantras. Therefore, Translator Renqin Sampo was a representative masters in the history of Tibetan Buddhism. The other famous translator of that time was Lekbe Sherap, who followed Master Artisa after he entered Tibet and was one of his three close disciples. We will give a detailed account of him later in the chapter on the Kardam Sects of Tibetan Buddhism.

Many Tibetan historical records have that not only stated that Lha Lama Yeshe O sent Buddhist monks of the Ngari area to Kashmir to study, but he but also invited many prominent foreign monks to the Tibetan areas. For instance, Pundit Dhamma Pala, a celebrated Buddhist monk from Tianzhu, together with his four close disciples, was invited to Tibet to preach monastic disciplines. Gya Weixirab, a monk of the Guge area, was ordained as a bhiksu by them. The tradition of monastic disciplines being handed down from the five

The Sutra Hall of the Chamzhub Monastery.

Indian eminent monks was called "the upper route of monastic disciplines".

In order to invite more Indian eminent monks to revive Buddhism, Lha Lama Yeshe O even went on an expedition for the cause of the Dharma. Unfortunately, in the course of his journey, he was captured by a neighboring Muslim king, who demanded a ransom equal to Yeshe O's weight in gold. Historical records show that Lha Lama Jangchub O, Yeshe O's great-nephew, collected as much gold that he possible could to gain the release of Yeshe O. (Lha Lama Jangchub O was one of three sons of Lhade, who was son of King Sungbei, Lha Lama Yeshe O's little brother. Sungbei ascended the throne after Lha Lama Yeshe O when the latter became a monk). But the gold Lha lama Jangchub O amassed was insufficient. When they met each other, Lha Lama Yeshe O told his great-nephew: "I am a very old man, and I have not yet had the opportunity to sacrifice my life for the Dharma. Don't give the gold to my captors and waste money on me. Use it instead to invite Master Artisa to Tibet." This was what Master Lha Lama Yeshe O had done near the end of his life, and later he died in prison. His long cherished wish, to invite Master Artisa to revive Dharma in Tibet, finally came to fruition through his follower's efforts.

Reluctantly, Lha Lama Jangchub O followed his great-uncle's advice, and sent Gyatsundru Senge and Nagtso Lotsawa, with a quantity of gold, to India to invite Master Artisa. After repeated setbacks, Master Artisa succeeded in entering Tibet. The great scholar once again caused the Dharma to flourish in Tibet and advanced the process of the revival of orthodox Buddhism. Thereafter, "the second dissemination period of Tibetan Buddhism" was launched

The Shekarqoide Monastery and the relics of the Shekarzong Monastery, both of which is built in the 17th century and located in Dingri County.

throughout Tibet. It was known that "the lower route spread of Tibetan Buddhism", characterized by inheriting the lineage of the monastic disciplines, while "the upper route spread of Buddhism" featured translating Buddhist scriptures. Whichever route one considers, they both contributed much to the revival of Tibetan Buddhism. It is as Shi Xian said: "the lower route spread of Buddhism" ignited the fire of Tibetan Buddhism in the second dissemination period of Buddhism, while "the upper route spread of Buddhism" fanned the fire into flames.

In addition, according to *History on Buddhism by Purdain*, during the time of Lha Lama Yeshe O, Indian translator Banmar Rize invited Pundit Medi and Chalha Rangpa to Tibet. But the translator happened to die of gastric disease as they reached Tibet. Because of the language barrier, the two pundits had to drift along from one place to another. At last, Pundit Medi settled in Dharna and was employed to graze sheep, where he was found by Cheshe Zhapa Somnain Gyaincain, who invited him to preach Dharma in Manlung. Somnai Gyaincain also built a preaching hall of Abhidharma-Kosa Sastra at Danlung. Pundit Medi became a Tibetan linguist, translating many Buddhist scriptures such as *Manjusri Wisdom Dharma Door*, *Vipasyn Buddha Secret Doctrines* and so on. At the Langqu Golden Hall, he also wrote Speech Commentary, which was not just a work on Buddhism, but also a linguistic guide to the vocabulary and sentence construction in both Sanskrit and Tibetan. It was also an authoritative work among Tibetan classic linguistic studies. With regard to Pundit Chalha Rangpa, only brief accounts can be found in available historic records, which mentioned that he imparted some secret meditation practices and Buddhist tantras to Rongpa Wusang.

During the period of King Lhade of the Guge kingdom, pundit Sakya Sheli was invited from Kashmir to spread Dharma in Tibet. During the time he stayed Tibet, many Buddhist scriptures as well as monastic disciplines were translated under his direction. The tradition handed down from Pundit Sakya Sheli was called Banqin monastic disciplines.

Comparatively, in the second period of dissemination, the development of Tibetan Buddhism surpassed that of its first dissemination period in terms of the sphere of influence, or the degree to which adherents worshiped the Dharma. Tibetan Buddhism in the second dissemination period went through a prolonged period, but on the largest scale ever. It experienced over 500 years from the 10th century to the earlier part of the 15th century when the Gelug Sect was established. In view of the evolvement of religious history, it was a flourishing period of Buddhism, as various Buddhist sects with different religious cultural characteristics were produced at that time. In addition, the Incarnation System of Living Buddha also appeared.

Most of Tibetan Buddhist sects, except the Gelug sect, came into being in succession during the period from 1057 to 1293, which indicated that it was a great time of development. Several reasons can be attributed to the flourishing of Buddhism in the Tibetan areas, such as a comparatively stable society, prosperous economy, as well as large numbers of eminent monks coming forward, together with dynamic religious activities.

During the ensuing time from the 13th century, Tibetan Buddhism began to spread to neighboring areas, ending its unitary circle of Tibetan culture and religion. It was a new splendid chapter for the development of Tibetan Buddhism. It has continued to be worshipped in China's Tibet Autono-

The statue of Sakyamuni worshiped in the Statue Hall behind the hall of Yonbo Lhakang.

The Potala Palace.

The elegant carving on the eave of Jokhang of Lhasa, which construction was started from 647.

The Gold Lamp on a bronze pedestal flanked by two sliver lamps kept in the Samye Monastery of Lhasa of the Tibetan Autonomous Region. These three gold or sliver lamps have a history of over 1200 years.

mous Region, as well as Qinghai, Gansu Sichuan and Yunnan provinces, and the Xinjiang Uygur and Inner Mongolia autonomous regions. Prolonged ethnic cultural exchanges also enabled Tibetan Buddhism to make its way into the Tibetan, Mongolian, Pumi, Yuga, Tu and other ethnic minorities throughout China. It has also made its way into Bhutan, Sikkim, Nepal, India, the Mongolian Peoples' Republic and some areas of Russia. Even some countries of Europe and North America have Buddhist worshippers and monasteries. Therefore, Tibetan Buddhism is not only an important component of Chinese Buddhism, but also one of the most influential religions in the world.

4.Buddhist Sects

Tibetan Buddhism, with its large influenced areas, various internal sects, large quantity of monasteries and monks, nuns and followers, not only has exerted profound and extensive influence on the fields of politics, the economy, culture and so on, but also made its way into neighboring nationalities.

Before the peaceful liberation of Tibet in 1951, and even before the Democratic Reform of 1959, Tibet had long been a society of feudal serfdom under the despotic religious/political rule of monks and nobles. Tibetan Buddhism dominated the ideology of Tibetan people, and the upper class of Buddhist monks directly engaged in state affairs, which went entirely beyond the normal functions of religion. It was not until the Democratic Reform that Tibet was able to abolish feudal serfdom and launch the necessary religious reforms to achieve a separation of religion and state. The Chinese government strictly implemented the policy of religious freedom, liberating the masses in the fields of ideology, culture, production and living. Statistics show that, before the Democratic Reform, in the Tibet autonomous region, there were altogether 2,711 Tibetan Buddhist monasteries of various sects, 114,103 Buddhist monks and nuns (including 4000 living Buddhas of the upper class), which accounted for the 10 percent of the entire population. Other Tibetan areas showed a similar proportion. For instance, in Qinghai Province, there were 722 Buddhist monasteries, 57,647 Buddhist monks and nuns (among them 1,240 living Buddhas); in Sichuan Province, 747 monasteries, 93,700 monks and nuns; in Gansu Province, 369 monasteries, 16,900 monks and nuns (310 living Buddhas); in the Diqin Tibetan Autonomous Prefecture of Yunnan Province, 3,233 monks and nuns, with 34 living Buddhas. The number of monasteries and monks and nuns in the Inner Mongolian and Xinjiang autonomous regions were not included. Altogether, there were 285,583 monks and nuns residing in 4,573 monasteries. With so many people not taking part in production activities, undeniably, they added a heavy economic burden on the local people of the Tibetan areas.

After the Democratic Reform, the politico-religion system was abolished in the Tibetan areas, and the freedom of religious belief actually became a personal affair. It was a historical reform in the history of Tibetan Buddhism.

The hereditary Abbot Qoini of the Lamanhin Monastery of Nyingchi County. Qoini, at the age of 50, is belonged to Menba ethnic group. According to tradition of Nyingma Sect (Red Sect), he had one son after marriage.

The elegant bronze bell kept in the Samye Monastery, was cast in the late years of the 8th century not long before the monastery was built. As a rare culture relic, the bell is the first one to be cast in the Tibetan Autonomous Region.

The Statue of Buddha worshiped in the Lamanyin Monastery in Nyingchi County.

A shopping store near the Samye Monastery, which is well known as "masterpiece in the history of construction".

According to statistics of 1965, about 553 monasteries and 6,913 monks and nuns still remained, which matched the actual situation of the Tibetan areas. The movement was a practice of national religious policy of the Chinese government on Tibet, with the result of not only liberating productive forces, but also satisfying the needs of followers of Tibetan Buddhism. During the period of the Cultural Revolution, in Tibet as in other parts of China, the policy on freedom of religious belief was disrupted, and the broad mass of adherents of Tibetan Buddhism were greatly hurt. Following the introduction of the open and reform policy of 1978, however, Tibetan Buddhist followers once again gained the right of freedom of religious belief, with a wave of reconstruction and renovation of Buddhist monasteries, and the re-emergence of monks and nuns throughout the Tibet Autonomous Region. This indirectly showed that Tibetan Buddhism was widely worshiped by fervent Tibetan people.

At present, Tibetan Buddhism has stepped onto a new historical stage with sound development. It has been in a stage of maturity and stability in terms of organizations of monasteries, monastic disciplines, as well as Buddhist activities. Latest statistics indicate that, in the Tibetan areas, which cover the Tibet Autonomous Region, Qinghai, Sichuan, Gansu and Yunnan provinces, there are altogether 2,769 monasteries, about half the number that existed before the Democratic Reform. As for the distribution or influence of different Buddhist sects, the Gelug Sect is the most extensive and influential, with 1,460 monasteries covering the Tibetan areas, around half the total number of monasteries of all Buddhist sects of Tibetan Buddhism. Its influence is represented by seven main monasteries, which include: three in Lhasa, namely the Gandain, Zhaibung and Sera monasteries, the capital remaining a sacred place for pilgrimage; the Tashilhungpo Monastery located in Xigaze, the resident monastery of the Panchen Lama, has won high prestige among Buddhist followers; the Qambarlhin Monastery in Qamdo, was the resident monastery of Living Buddha Pabalha and has exerted influence in the locality; the

The Lamanyin Monastery in Nyingchi County, which was built in 1925 and belonged to the Nyingma Sect (Red Sect).

Tar Monastery in Hungzong county of Qinghai province, was the place where Master Tsongkapa was born; the Labrang Monastery in Shahe county of Gansu Province, the resident monastery of Living Buddha Jamyang, has great influence among Buddhist worshipers in the Tibetan areas of Gansu, Qinghai and Sichuan provinces. Generally speaking, the Gelug Sect mainly enjoys influence in the Tibet Autonomous Region, followed by the Tibetan areas of Qinghai and Gansu provinces.

The Niyngma Sect was the second most influential sect, with 753 monasteries covering the Tibet Autonomous Region, Sichuan, Qinghai, Gansu, and Yunnan provinces. Among them, the Ganzi and Arbe areas of Sichuan Province were its main sphere of influence, represented by Garto Monastery, the White Jade Monastery and Zoqin Monastery. The Tibet Autonomous Region, where the Nyingma Sect originated, also has its influence, with the Mincholhin and Dorjezha monasteries as its most representative.

The Kargyu Sect at present has 366 monasteries covering the Tibetan areas, with the Tibet Autonomous Region and the Yushu Prefecture of Qinghai Province as its two main centers of activity. It is third in terms of scale and influence.

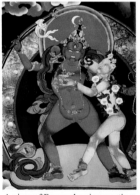

A piece of Fresco showing practices of Tantracism, which is kept in the Chosung Monastery at the Island of Barsungcho Lake of Gongbogyamdar County. The Chosung Monastery is belonged to the Nyingma Sect of Tibetan Buddhism.

The Statue of Master Artisa at Choma Lhakang of Qoishi. The Choma Lhakang was built in the 11th century when Master Artisa spread Buddhism there. The stupa for Master Artisa was built after attained parinirvana.

The Sakya Sect has 141 monasteries, with the Sakya Monastery as its ancestral and representative one. Its influence was limited in the Tibet Autonomous Region. In addition, the Gyunam Sect has 37 monasteries, mainly distributed in the Arbe Prefecture of Sichuan Province and the Golo Prefecture of Qinghai Province, with the Ramtan Monastery as its main representatives. With regard to other Buddhist sects, such as the Kardam, Shigye, Gyoyu and Bulug, they exist in the Tibetan areas only as theoretical and not practical sects.

1). The Nyingma Sect

The Nyingma Sect has the longest history among all the sects of Tibetan Buddhism. "Nyingma" literally means "ancient" or "old", thus the "Nyingma Sect" means "the old sect". Its name traces back to the Indian master, Guru Padmasambhava, also known as Guru Rinpoche, who came to Tibet in 817 at the invitation of King Trisong Detsan. The Nyingma Sect was said to carry on tantric teachings as well as related practices and rituals, which were handed down from "the first dissemination period of Tibetan Buddhism". The sect is also known as the "Red Sect" or "Red Hat Sect", for the red hat that eminent monks used to wear, but it does not seem to be an appropriate title.

As an independent sect, Nyingma was formed in "the second dissemination period of Tibetan Buddhism", as no sects were formed in "the first dissemination period of Tibetan Buddhism". In its early days, tantric teachings were handed down orally from father to son or teacher to close disciple, so the Nyingma Sect did not form a unified systematic doctrine, as well as established and authoritative monasteries, thus leading to a relaxed monastic institution. Although the teachings and lineage of the Nyingma Sect are comparatively complex, they fall into three transmission lineages: Kama, namely Oral Transmission Lineage; II. Terma, namely Concealed Treasures Transmission lineage; III. Daknang, Visionary Lineage.

In the early stage of "the second dissemination period of

The inner view of stupa for Master Artisa at Choma Lhakang of Qoishui.

Tibetan Buddhism", three masters crucial to the formation of the Nyingma Sect deserve special mention. They are historically called the "Three Master Sois", namely Soipoqeb Sakyaqoinam, Soiqoi Xirabzhaba, Soi Sakyasanga. Master Soipoqeb Sakyaqoinam, from his childhood, followed many tantric masters at that time, and learned extensive texts of the Nyingma Sect, gradually grasping various tantric doctrines popular at that time. For instance, he followed Master Nang Yexe Qoinam and studied the Imaginary Tantra, and then Master Togar Namkala imparted to him the Collection of Tantras. As the result, Soipoqeb Sakyaqoinam basically learned all the tantric teachings handed down from the distant lineage of Buddhist scriptures. Later, Soipoqeb Sakyaqoinam presented Great Master Chomi Sakyayeshe with 100 tael of gold, in return learning the Path to the Great Perfection. After various instructions of great masters of the Nyingma Sect and through his own hard work, Soipoqeb Sakyaqoinam rose to be a famous master with good command of the doctrines of the Nyingma Sect and one immersed in religious knowledge. What deserves mention is that he established the Wobalhung Monastery, setting up a unified center of religious activities for the Nyingma Sect. From then on, Master Soipoqeb Sakyaqoinam set out to launch a series of religious activities to develop the doctrines of the Nyingma Sect. It was a new era for the sect, as the establishment of

A piece of fresco of the Chosung Monastery of the Nyingma Sect of Tibetan Buddhism. The monastery is located at the Island of Barsungcho Lake of Gongbogyamdar County.

Lamas reciting Buddhist scriptures on the sutra hall of Choma Lhakang of Qoishi.

the Wobalhung Monastery allowed it to join the line of regular monasteries with complete teachings and rituals as well as a monastery institution, ending its former scattered structure and non-institutional condition.

When Master Soipoqeb Sakyaqoinam passed away, Soiqoi Xirabzhaba succeeded him. He, in turn established and completed the regulations and institutions of the monasteries, as he took in charge of the Wobalhung and Chopo monasteries and the meditation place of Zhagyewo, ensuring their religious activities took on a regular form, For instance, he ordered that religious activities in the Wobalhung Monastery should be held in the morning, at noon in the Chopo Monastery, and in the evening at Zhagyewo. At the same time, in order to expand the scale of religious activities, he presided over the construction of a grand temple, named the Air Flying Temple, which was supported by nine main pillars. Altogether, 42 statues of Buddha were housed there; on the walls were paintings of the Mandala. Other small temples were also built at that time. Master Soiqoi Xirabzhaba made great achievements in the theory of Buddhist Tantra, especially in Buddhist Logic. Famous for his great debating ability, he came to be one of the main rivals of many Buddhist monks from the newly rising sects of Tibetan Buddhism when they debated the scriptures. As he was always victorious and gained great prestige, many his rivals in the end willingly became his disciples. Because a large number of Buddhist monks of the Nyingma Sect at that time were laymen, rather than ordained monks, they put more emphasis on the practice of Tantricism, instead of the study of Sutric theory. On the condition that there were quite limited talents in good command of debate in Buddhist Tantras in the Nyingma Sect, Master Soiqoi Xirabzhaba distinguished himself and made an important contribution to the good image of the Nyingma Sect among other Buddhist sects.

Soi Sakyasanga, also known as Lhagyiqinbo Chopoba, was born in1074, when his father, Master Soiqoi Xirabzhaba died. Historical Tibetan records show that Master Soiqoi Xirabzhaba had three sons and several daughters, who were all Buddhist monks or nuns practicing the doctrines of the Nyingma Sect. Master Soi Sakyasanga, the last son, was the only one to make great achievements and continue his father's cause. He was brought up by his mother and uncle to manage family affairs as he learned much knowledge at home before the age of fifteen. At that time, the family was well off so that someone needed to be in charge of family affairs. In the following four years from the age of fifteen, Soi Sakyasanga left home to follow one master or another, systematically learning Buddhist sutras and Tantras, especially all the tantric teachings of distant lineage of the Nyingma Sect. In the end, he became the successor of this lineage. Chopo Monastery, as his place of residence, was reconstructed and renovated on a large scale. It usually held large-scale religious activities four times every year, namely spring, summer, autumn, and winter gatherings. In 1134, Soi Sakyasanga passed away at the age of 60. In his brief life, he contributed to furthering the formal monastery development of the Nyingma Sect, successfully completing the tasks and responsibilities of an occupational Buddhist master.

Due to the ceaseless efforts of the three masters, the Nyingma Sect had evolved into an independent sect with established monasteries, systematic Buddhist classics and fixed monastic institutions. It also won a certain prestige at that time. The lineage belonged to the distant Buddhist classics lineage, which is the most orthodox and authoritative lineage and is still being handed down.

Besides the three masters above, there is another figure that made a special contribution to the development of the Nyingma Sect., namely Lhungqin Rabgyamba, born in 1308

The statue of 1000-eyed Buddha in the Samye Monastery.

The statue of Sakyamuni worshiped at the Buddha Hall behind the Wuzi Great Hall of the Samye Monastery. It was carved from one huge rock from Mountain Habo, and the statue is 3.9 meters in height, 1.8 meters in the width of shoulder. The statue is one of rarest crafts in the early stage of Buddha carving.

Lampe ‡ beurre de yack en or.

with the name of Zimei Aosei. At the age of twelve, he became a Buddhist monk and studied tantric teachings before many masters of the Nyingma Sect and other sects at that time. He also studied the *Five Sutras by Maitreya*, *Seven Sutras of Buddhist Logic by Dharmak* and other Tantras. Therefore, Lhungqin Rabgyamba came to be a famous master proficient in tantric and sutric teachings. He was a prolific master and his most important works are *35 Kinds of Nyingti Practices* and *Seven Tibetan Commentaries*, which mainly expounded the teachings of Great Perfection, the highest stage of practice of the Nyingma Sect. In his later years, he lectured on another profound Tantra, the Flying Air Nyingti, and contributed much to its dissemination, before dying in 1363 at the age of 56.

In his short life, Master Lhungqin Rabgyamba not only completed and developed the teachings and doctrines of the Nyingma Sect, but also cultivated many famous Buddhist monks. He played a crucial role in the expansion of the sect's influence. He also visited Bhutan, where he built the Tarbalin Monastery, and that led to the eventual spread of the Nyingma Sect, to Nepal. Eventually, many Buddhist monks from Bhutan and Nepal came to Choqin Monastery to learn the teachings of the Nyingma Sect.

The Nyingma Sect further developed in the 17th century under the patronage of the 5th Dalai. He not only supported the sect's original monasteries, promoting the influence of Dorjezha Monastery and Minchulhin Monastery, but also built in person a new monastery called the Monastery of Longevity Continent for imparting the teachings of the Nyingma Sect. He also ordered the transformation of Lhalung Monastery in Lozha, in the Shannan area, built by Dusung Qenba, the founder of the Kharma Kargyu sect, into a monastery of the Nyingma Sect. Furthermore, the social position of the Nyingma Sect greatly improved at that time. Since the period of the 5th Dalai, the local government of Tibet used to invite Buddhist monks of the Nyingma Sect to practice divination and help them when they encountered war and other turmoil, natural disasters, plague and so on.

Therefore, during the time of the 5th Dalai, the influence and development of the Nyingma Sect reached its zenith.

At present, there are altogether 753 Buddhist monasteries of the Nyingma Sect throughout the Tibetan areas of China, second only to the Gelug Sect among all the sects of Tibetan Buddhism. As a sect with the longest history, it has undergone a prolonged historical process of evolution. As we know, a batch of famous monasteries, including Samye monastery in the Tibet Autonomous Region, were built in the 8th century. But this was not enough for the Nyingma Sect, and there were also many other old monasteries in the Tibetan areas. For instance, Master Birocana, one of the first batch of Buddhist monks in "the first dissemination period of Tibetan Buddhism", went to promote Buddhism to today's Arba Tibetan area of Sichuan province in the 8th century. He did much to propagate Buddhism there: He translated foreign Buddhist scriptures into Tibetan, practiced meditation, imparted Buddhist doctrines to local disciples, and made efforts to build monasteries. Due to his great efforts, the Arba Tibetan area saw a flourishing of Tibetan Buddhism of the Nyingma Sect, with more monasteries than any other sect, a unique phenomenon in areas influenced by Tibetan Buddhism. So, the Nyingma Sect not only has a long history in the Arba Tibetan area, but also great influence there.

In addition, Tubo Buddhism, predecessor of the Nyingma Sect, was introduced in succession into the Diqen Tibetan area of Yunnan province in the 8th century. Although at present the number of the Buddhist monasteries of the Nyingma Sect stands only the third there, it was the place where the sect was first introduced into Tibetan areas.

Tubo Buddhism was introduced into Qinghai Tibetan areas in the 9th century. In 841, when King Lhang Dharma launched a move to suppress Buddhism, three

The statues of guardian deities in the Samye Monastery.

The former Abbots of the Nyingma Sect (Red Sect) of the Samye Monastery.

The Mandala fresco in the Samye Monastery.

Tibetan Buddhist monks, namely Mar Shakya Yeshi, Yogejung and Tsang Rabsel, fled to the Tibetan areas in the eastern part of Qinghai Province, taking with them many Buddhist sutras on monastic disciplines. They made great contributions to preventing the Dharma from disappearing. They lectured on Buddhism and cultivated Buddhist disciples in Gyanzha county of Hongnam Tibetan Autonomous Prefecture and in the Haiton areas, such as Shenho, Holhung, Huzhu, Lhedo, Xining and so on. Many monasteries were built at that time as centers of religious activities, including Dando Monastery and White Horse Monastery. At present, many monasteries of the Nyingma Sect are found throughout the Tibetan areas of Qinghai province, second in number to the Gelug Sect.

The monasteries of the Nyingma Sect mainly cover four provinces: the Tibetan Autonomous Region, with 344 monasteries; Ganzi and Arbe of Sichuan Province, with 262 monasteries; Tibetan areas of Gansu Province, with eight monasteries and Diqen Tibetan area of Yunnan Province, with four monasteries. The figures above clearly show that monasteries of the Nyingma Sect mainly distributed in the Tibet Autonomous Region and Sichuan Province. In terms of time of construction, several monasteries such as Samye Monastery were built during "the first dissemination period of Tibetan Buddhism", while a large number were built during "the second dissemination period of Tibetan Buddhism". So other sects' monasteries in the course of construction influenced the monasteries of the Nyingma Sect. At present, many monasteries of the Nyingma Sect, whether in terms of construction scale or of monastic institution, can match those of other sects, even of the Gelug Sect - such as Karto, Choqin and White Jade monasteries of the Ganzi area of Sichuan Province, and Samye, Minchulhin and Dorjezha monasteries of the Shannan area of the Tibet Autonomous Region.

Karto Monastery, located 20 kilometers north of White Jade County of the Ganzi Tibetan prefecture of Sichuan Province, was a monastery with a long history. It was built by Eminent Monk Gardampa Desheshiba, a disciple of Mas-

A piece of fresco showing the paintings of two Bodhisattavas in the Samye Monastery.

A piece of fresco of the Samye Monastery.

ter Chopuba, one of three master Sois of the Nyingma Sect, in the middle of the 12th century. In its heyday, Karto Monastery occupied an area of 1,000,000 square meters, and had 48 sutra-reciting halls, 42 sutra-debating halls, and 513 residential houses for Buddhist monks. The monastery also had 11 sutra-printing halls, where over 900 Buddhist scriptures in Tibetan or Sanskrit were housed. The most famous buildings were its three Buddha temples: The first temple housed a bronze stupa from India, with a height of 9.4 meters; the second temple housed a bronze statue of Buddha Sakyamuni, with a height of 8 meters; and the third temple was a tantric temple. In terms of succession of Buddhist teachings and rituals, Karto Monastery imparted what belonged to the Minchulhin School called "Southern Lineage", as well as "the Distant Lineage of Buddhist Scriptures" of the Nyingma Sect. The Abbot of the monastery succeeded under the system of "Reincarnation of the Living Buddha". Generally speaking, Karto Monastery was an established monastery of the Nyingma Sect, with a large scale, complete equipment and structure. Before the peaceful liberation of 1959, under the patronage of Tusi Dege, Karto Monastery furthered its development and influence and gained higher prestige in the Tibetan areas, leading to ceaseless worshipers going to pay homage. Today, after large-scale reconstruction and renovation directed by the Chinese government, Karto Monastery has

A piece of fresco in the Samye Monastery showing wrestling.

A piece of fresco in the Samye Monastery showing Sakyamuni lecturing Buddhist scriptures.

resumed its former splendid and is thriving.

In 1675, the White Jade Monastery was built by an eminent monk called Renzengungsam Xirab, near White Jade County of the Ganzi area in Sichuan Province and became another famous monastery of the Nyingma Sect. The monastery is characterized by its teachings and practices of Buddhist sutras and Tantras, which is different from other establishments of the Nyingma Sect. It has some relationship to the teachings and rituals of the Marcangpa sub-sect of the Pachu Kargyu Sect of Tibetan Buddhism. For instance, although the Abbot of the White Jade Monastery was chosen through the system of Reincarnation of the Living Buddha, they had to go to Dege Barbang Monastery of the Karma Kargyu Sect to receive ordination from Living Buddha Situ. Here it should be explained that Barbang Monastery, the ancestral temple of Tusi Dege, held a special position in the areas of Tusi Dege. So, there had been particular political and cultural background with regard to the phenomenon that the Buddhist teachings and rituals of the Nyingma Sect were merged with that of the Kargyu Sect. Nonetheless, White Jade Monastery has always been regarded as being of the Nyingma Sect, and has many sub-monasteries. Related materials have it that the White Jade Monastery owns over 100 sub-monasteries of the Nyingma Sect in many Tibetan areas, such as the Arba and Ganzi areas of Sichuan Province, Gyamda in the Qamdo area of the Tibet Autonomous Region,

The sutra hall of Wuzi Great Hall of the Samye Monastery.

Golo of Qinghai Province and so on. So, it is clear that White Jade Monastery is of crucial importance throughout Tibetan areas.

In 1684, the fifth Dalai Lama Arwan Lobsang Gyacho ordered his disciple Baima Renzem, a great scholar and eminent Buddhist monk of the Nyingma Sect, to go to the area of Kam to spread Buddhism. With the support of Tusi Lhinchong and Tusi Dege, Master Baima Renzem constructed Choqin Monastery northeast of Dege. Master Baima Renzem, the abbot of the Choqin Monastery, was posthumously admitted as its first Living Buddha. Thanks to various degree of support from the central government of the Qing Dynasty, local forces and neighboring countries, Choqin Monastery rose to become a most famous monastery of the Nyingma Sect in the area of Shikam, with its scale and speed of development and other aspects exceeding that of Karto and White Jade monasteries. Sichuan Province Archives show that, "in the ninth year of King Yongzheng of the Qing Dynasty (1731), Prince Go came to the area of Kam, and presented 100 statues of gilded Buddha. The third Renboqin, whose mother was Dala's aunt, established a sutra-preaching monastery financed by the forces of Tibet. Bhutan sent its Buddhist monks to study scriptures, and engaged with much money the first Lama of the monastery as its state master. The fifth Renboqin received the donation from Bhutan, and set up a senior sutra-preaching monastery and accommodated those who studied in the monastery without charge. Due to various support and assistance, Choqin Monastery developed with great speed and came to be the most important of the three monasteries of the Nyingma Sect in the Tibetan areas of Sichuan province." The words above show how Choqin Monastery flourished, and, meanwhile, Choqin itself did much to contribute to the development of the Nyingma Sect.

The paintings of Guru Padmasambhava, the forefather of the Nyingma Sect (Red Sect).

The Buddhist banners and Mani clay heap in a desert of the Ngari area of the Tibetan Autonomous Region.

For instance, in the teachings of Buddhism, it took after what the Gelug Sect had achieved in systematic study of the theory of Buddhist sutras, offering 13 compulsory courses of Buddhist scriptures of the Open School of Tibetan Buddhism, which was equal to the five sutras of that learned in the Gelug Sect. In addition, it taught the works of Master Lhungqin Jamraba and other famous scholars of the Nyingma Sect.

Therefore, the Choqin Monastery came to be the central monastery where teachings of the Nyingma Sect were systematically imparted in the Ganzi, Arba areas, even throughout the Tibetan areas. It even turned into the highest institution for attaining advanced Buddhist knowledge and study Tibetan traditional culture. Before the peaceful liberation of 1959, it housed 500-600 resident monks, and "it seemed that its prestige had surpassed that of the Dorjezha Monastery and the Minchulhin Monastery in the Lhasa areas." "Buddhist monks of the Nyingma Sect from various places went here for study, and among of them included Buddhist monks from Bhutan and Nepal." Therefore, the Choqin Monastery has won high prestige not only throughout the Tibetan areas of the People's Republic of China, but also in neighboring countries. As far as in the Tibetan areas of PRC is concerned, there are altogether over 100 sub-monasteries of the Nyingma Sect of Tibetan Buddhism, mainly covering the Arba and Ganzi areas of Sichuan Province, and the Yushu area of Qinghai Province.

As the place where Tibetan Buddhism originated and flourished, the Tibet Autonomous Region owned a large number of monasteries of various sects, which was unrivalled throughout the Tibetan areas. As far as the Nyingma Sect is concerned, the Dorjezha and Minchulhin monasteries have exerted great influence not only in the Tibet Autonomous Region, but also throughout the Tibetan areas.

The Dorjezha Monastery was located on the foot of a

cliff on the northern bank of the Yarlung Tsangpo River, in Gonggar County of the Shannan area. Seen from a distance, the medium-scale monastery blends well with the cliff, constituting a grand landscape. Dorjezha Monastery was said to have been built by a noble called Zhaxi Dorje whose family had been in decline. Dorjezha, in Tibetan literally means Diamond Cliff, originated from a green stone called Varja naturally produced on the cliff at the back of the monastery, hence the monastery's name. After its construction, especially owing to the strong support of the fifth Dalai Lama, Dorjezha Monastery developed with great speed. At its height, it housed over 2,000 resident monks, which was rare in the monasteries of the Nyingma Sect. The monastery was destroyed in the Cultural Revolution, and after the third plenary session of the eleventh Central Committee of Communist Party of China (CPC) in 1978, the central government earmarked much money to be used in its reconstruction and renovation. Living Buddha Dorjezha Jambeilobsung, deputy chairman of the Chinese People's Political Consultative Committee (CPPCC) of the Tibet Autonomous Region, and deputy director of Chinese Buddhism Committee, usually went to Dorjezha Monastery to preside over Buddhist activities. At present, the Dorjezha Monastery manages well, and most of its 29 monks are aged between 16 and 30, with only two old monks, respectively aged 71 and 77. All the monks, except one from Renbo County of Xigaze, are natives of Gonggar County. Dorjezha Monastery has a strict institution system. It set up the Democratic Management Commission of the Dorjezha Monastery in charge of its finances, religious activities, and daily affairs. The commission is composed of one director, two deputy directors and

A beautiful corner of the Ryezhen Monastery in Lhinzho County, which was built in 1057 by Zongtonpa, one of disciples of Master Artisa. Later, the Kardam Sect was developed on the foundation of the monastery.

95

Guardian deities of Sorcerers' Dance of the Ryezhen Monastery.

three members, and every one has his responsibility. With regard to its teaching lineage, it calls itself the ancestral monastery of the Northern Lineage of the Nyingma Sect of Tibetan Buddhism, with many sub-monasteries all around the Tibetan areas, especially Sichuan Province. Dorjezha Monastery has kept close relations with Choqin Monastery, which is in Dege County of the Ganzi area of Sichuan Province. As both of the monasteries belong to the Northern Lineage of the Nyingma Sect, Dorjezha and Choqin monasteries share similar Buddhist teachings, doctrines and religious rituals, and at the same time, they have learned from each other to offset their respective weakness. At present, in practical use of the Buddhist teachings and rituals, especially grasp of Buddhist knowledge, Dorjezha Monastery lags far behind Choqin Monastery, so the former often engages many eminent monks from the latter as teachers to raise the general standard of religious and cultural knowledge of its monks. Generally speaking, as one out of two monasteries of the Nyingma Sect with the highest prestige in the Tibet Autonomous Region (the other is the Mincholhing Monastery), Dorjezha Monastery not only has a high reputation among adherents in the Tibetan Autonomous Region, but has also exerted a certain influence throughout the Tibetan area. It is worth noting that the Abbot of Dorjezha Monastery succeeded according to the system of Reincarnation of the Living Buddha, and the title of Dorjezha Monastery was respectfully called "Renchenqinmo Dorjezha Jambeilobsam Gyinmeinamzogyacho". The present Living Buddha is the tenth Living Buddha Rechenqinmo Dorjezha Jambeilobsam, whose rank in the CPPCC of the Tibet

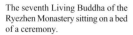
The seventh Living Buddha of the Ryezhen Monastery sitting on a bed of a ceremony.

Lamas of the Ryezhen Monastery playing Buddhist conch before a religious ceremony.

Autonomous Region indicates the concern and hope of the Chinese Communist Party and central government towards Dorjezha Monastery.

Mincholhin Monastery, located in Zhache Village of Zhanam County in the Shannan area, was famous for the succession and propagation of teachings of the Southern Lineage of the Nyingma Sect in the Tibetan areas. In was built in 1676 by Master Dedalhiba, who once served as the fifth Dalai Lama's teacher imparting to him the terma (Concealed Treasure) of the Nyingma Sect. Apart from spreading the teachings and rituals of the Southern Lineage, Mincholhin Monastery was celebrated for its study of the "Ten Treatises of Buddhism Doctrines", which covers the whole system of Tibetan traditional culture, including Rhetoric, Worlds and Expressions, Syntax, Drama, Astrology, Technology, Medicine, Grammar, Logic and Philosophy. It deserves mention that Mincholhin Monastery distinguishes itself from other monasteries of the Nyingma Sect, which tent to emphasize religious practices and meditations while belittling the importance of the study of Buddhist theory. Mincholhin Monastery, particularly, not only attaches great importance to the general grasp of theoretical knowledge of Tibetan Buddhism, but also makes efforts to probe Tibetan traditional culture systematically and has attained great achievements. Thus, Mincholhin Monastery became a comprehensive university on Tibetan Buddhism, not only probing Tibetan traditional culture but also going beyond the sphere of religious culture. Before the peaceful liberation of Tibet in 1951, innumerable monks from other areas were attracted to Mincholhing Monastery to study because of its reputation, including many officials of local governments who were attracted to learn Tibetan traditional culture. Therefore, it seems that its contribution to the prosperity and development of Tibetan traditional culture is far greater than the role it played in the development of the Nyingma Sect itself. For instance, the handwriting skill that Mincholhin Monastery achieved was well known. This influenced Tibetan calligraphers over many generations, and greatly furthered the development of the cause of Tibetan calligraphy. In addition, in the 18th to the 19th centuries, there arose many eminent Buddhist monks of the Nyingma Sect who were proficient in the "Ten Treatises of Buddhism Doctrines" and created high achievements in Tibetan traditional culture, which obviously advanced the good environment for studying Tibetan traditional culture that the Mincholhin Monastery had created and advocated.

At present, it has 53 resident monks, with five aged from 45 to 74; and the others ranging in age from 17 to 34. Among them, except for two who are respectively from Chomei and Samri counties, all are natives of Zhanam County. The monastery is managed democratically and composed of a chief director, deputy director and members. It still maintains its advantage in advocating and promoting the good tradition of studying Tibet traditional culture.

The Samye Monastery, as we know, is presided over by the Nyingma, Sagya, and Gelug sects. The guardian halls of the Nyingma and Sagya sects house respectively the sacred guardian deities of the two sects, showing they not only possess their own powers within the monastery, but also take responsibility to protect its dignity and authority. Within the sharing arrangement, there is no priority in terms of religious rituals, which means that each of the three sects has equal rights. Rituals are staged based mainly on a collective decision by followers of the three sects. Therefore, from the viewpoint of the monastery itself, the lines between the sects are definitely blurred.

As is well known, Jokhang is a celebrated monastery of Tibetan Buddhism at home and abroad. In the view of history, Jokhang was among the first batch of temples built during the reign of King Songtsan Gampo, so it can be regarded as

The Sakgya Monastery, located at the foot of Mountain Pobori, has stood over 900 years since 1073 when it was constructed.

Lamas of the Sakgya Monastery inviting various gods and deities out of the temple before Sorcerers' Dance.

of the Nyingma Sect. The Jokhang is listed as one of the national important culture relics under special protection, and it has been rebuilt and renovated many times by the local and central Chinese government. Among the mass followers of Tibetan Buddhism, the Samye Monastery, especially the Statues of Buddha Sakyamuni housed in the temple, has enjoyed a sacred and pre-eminent position. Hence, Jokhang has become a sacred temple dominating the various sects of Tibetan Buddhism, without distinct dividing lines between them. Here it is worth noting that in 1409, Master Tsongkapa, the founder of the Gelug Sect, successfully held in Jokhang the Grand Prayer Ceremony, the largest ever in terms of scale, content and significance, and thereafter, the Gelug Sect has continued the tradition to hold large-scale ceremonies until today. Although the Gelug Sect naturally became the sect managing the daily affairs of Jokhang, because of good timing, geographical convenience and harmonious human relations it developed, nevertheless there is no distinct idea of sects in the Jokhang. Not only are many principal Buddhas and guardian deities worshiped there, but it also has many statues of eminent monks of various sects of Tibetan Buddhism as well as paintings related to them. Around the temple are the halls of various sects of Tibetan Buddhism, packed with worshipers at every season. At any time, every influential sect can hold its religious rituals and activities there. Every year, millions of Buddhist adherents have come to Jokhang to pay homage, along with innumerable disciples and tourists. Although the Samye, Jokhang and Chamzhub monasteries are composite monasteries blending various sects of Tibetan Buddhism, among disciples of the Nyingma Sect, even eminent monks through the generations, share the unswerving view that the three monasteries mentioned above are their ancestral monasteries, which is of great importance to the Nyingma Sect.

Taking a panoramic view of the 700 Buddhist monasteries of the Nyingma Sect, it is not difficult to conclude that the Nyingma Sect has played a crucial role in the field of Tibetan Buddhism. It has a great influence among the mass adherents of Tibetan Buddhism in the Tibetan areas, especially among the common people, which is second only to the Gelug Sect.

2). The Kardam Sect

The Kardam Sect was an earlier sect formed in Tibetan Buddhism. Here in Tibetan "Kar" means "Buddhism", and

The Guardian Deities' Dance in winter of the Sakgya Monastery.

"dams" means "teach". The word "Kardam" therefore referred to using Buddhist scriptures to guide ordinary people's behavior. As for its meaning, Master Tukan Qoigyinyima explained in his book Different Sects and Doctrines of Tibetan Buddhism: The sect incorporated teachings of Buddha Tathagata into that of Master Artisa, who advocated gradual practice as the route to the Great Perfection, hence the sect's name. Generally speaking, the Kardam Sect of Tibetan Buddhism was initiated by Master Artisa, developed by Zongtonpa, the favorite disciple of Atisa, and promoted by their successors. In the 15th century, with the rise of the Gelug Sect, the Kardam Sect was annexed and in the end disappeared as an independent entity.

Master Atisa, also known as Precious Lord, took the ordination name Dipamkara Srijhana. In 1042,he left Vikramashila Monastery of India for the western region of Tibet at the invitation of Lha Lama Yeshe O, King of the Guge Kingdom. In the following three years, Master Artisa devoted himself to spreading Buddhism in the Ngari area and gained great respect from local believers. At that time, admiring Master Artisa's reputation, many Buddhist disciples and followers from the central areas of Tibet were attracted to his side and strove to invite him to their home area to spread Buddhism. Therefore, against his wishes, as he had planned to return to Vikramashila Monastery, Master Artisa took up the invitation of Zongtonpa, and reached the central areas of Tibet after spending three years in the Ngari area. From then on, Zongtonpa followed Master Artisa and became a close disciple. Master Artisa stayed in many Tibetan Buddhist monasteries, such as Samye Monastery, Nyetang Monastery and so on. He preached Buddhist doctrines and dealt with problems in a broad and effective way wherever he went. He also spared no pains to hold enshrining ceremony for quite a number of monasteries, Buddhist pagodas and Buddhism Statues, as well as accepting many disciples; he held initiation ceremonies for them and imparted all kinds of ways to study Buddhist sutras. In 1054, at the age of 73, Master Artisa hadn't returned India as his

A piece of Fresco in the Sakgya Monastery.

wished and died at the Nyetang Monastery, several kilometers southwest of Lhasa. He had traveled for about 13 years in Tibetan areas and spread Buddhism wherever he went, playing an important role in promoting and flourishing Buddhism in the western and central areas.

Master Artisa translated and wrote many scriptures on open and secret schools of Tibetan Buddhism while he stayed in Tibet. The most important work is *The Lamp that Shows the Path to Enlightenment*, which is a classic that lays down a foundation for the teachings of the Kardam Sect. As a canon merged with Tantras (scriptures of the secret school of Tibetan Buddhism) and sutras (scriptures of the open school of Tibetan Buddhism) of the Mahayana theory, it elaborated that there should be no conflicts between them; instead, they should always compromise. At the same time, one should practice Buddhism step by step. The works provided a theoretical foundation for Master Tsongkapa's two famous classics, *The Gradual Way to Bodhisattva* and *The Gradual Way to Tantricism*.

Another important achievement of Master Artisa is that he trained and cultivated four famous disciples, namely Nyachocechengyiwa, Kutunzunziyongdrong, Erlebeixirab, Zongtunbaviqoinnei. Among of them, Zongtonpa, his favorite disciple, absorbed all the teachings of the open and secret schools of Tibetan Buddhism, and set up a theoretical system for the teachings of the Kardam Sect.

Zongtonpa was born into a wealthy family of Duilhung. He was well educated in his childhood and started to learn Buddhism as he grew up. In 1045, he left for Ngari to invite Master Artisa to central Tibet to promote the spread

The statue of Saqin Gonggar Nyingbo.

of Buddhism, and from then on he followed the Master until he died at Nyetang Monastery. Zongtonpa fully deserved to be the most senior among many disciples of Master Artisa. In 1055, he presided over the Grand Summons Ceremony commemorating the first anniversary of Artisa's parinirvana in Nyetang, and built a monastery called Nyetang. In 1057, with the support of the feudal head of the Damxung area in northern Tibet, Zongtonpa established a monastery at Ryezhen, giving its name to the Ryezhen Monastery. With this as its fundamental religious site, the Kardam Sect of Tibetan Buddhism gradually formed.

After the death of Zongtonpa, the post of Chief Abbot of Ryezhen Monastery was occupied by Namjor Qinbo, another disciple of Master Artisa, who was succeeded by Kongbawa, also a disciple of the great master. After that, the Chief Abbot's

A piece of fresco in the Sakgya Monastery.

post of Ryezhen Monastery was occupied in succession by the disciples of Zongtonpa. There are three famous figures, namely Bodorwa Reqinsei, Gyinewa Cechenba and Puqoinwa Shanno Gyaincain. They and their successors built many monasteries. Bodorwa built Bodor Monastery; Chaqoikarba, an eminent monk of the Kardam Sect, and a disciple of Bodorwa, established Qoikar Monastery at Mozhu near Lhasa; in 1164, Sei Gyibopa constructed a new monastery near Qoikar Monastery, known as Gyibo Monastery; Tundain built Nyatang Monastery in 1153, in 1073, Erleibixirab, one of the disciples of Master Artisa, constructed a monastery, at first known as the Nyeto Monastery but later called Sampo Monastery. In addition, there are many other monasteries of the Kardam Sect such as Gyiayu, Lo, Ganggang and Renqingang.

Among many monasteries of the Kardam Sect, except Ryezhen Monastery, there are still two influential monasteries today, namely the Sampo and Nyatang monasteries. Sampo Monastery, located south of Lhasa and east of Nyetang, is famous for advocating Buddhist debate and Hetuvidya

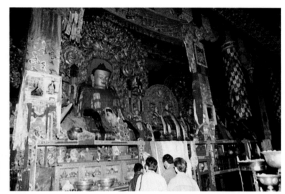

Followers of Tibetan Buddhism worshiped Buddha Sakyamuni in the Sakgya Monastery.

(Buddhist Logic), which held an important position in the history of Tibetan Buddhism. Nyetang Monastery is the earliest place to edit and revise *Gangyur* and *Dangyur* of the *Tripitaka* in Tibetan, also called the Nyetang edition, for which the Nyetang Monastery is famous. In 1409, Master Tsongkapa established the Gelug Sect, on the basis of the doctrines and rituals of the Kardam Sect. Gradually, many monasteries and monks of the Kardam Sect were forced to convert to the Gelug Sect, which earned it another name as the new Kardam Sect. Thereupon, the Kardam Sect vanished as an independent sect in Tibetan areas.

3). The Sagya Sect

The Sagya Sect is one of important of Tibetan Buddhism. Its founder is known as Kun Gongqoi Gyibo, decedent of the Noble Kuns in the Tubo Kingdom. This was an eminent family with long succession following the tradition of the Nyingma Sect, and making significant contribution to the formation and development of Tibetan Buddhism. The Sagya Sect takes pride in the fact that Kun Lhuyi Wangbosung, son of Kun Banpoche (Prime Minister of Tsampos Trisong Detsan of the Tubo Kingdom), was the first monk of the Kuns and one of the earliest seven monks of Tubo, as well as the first batch of monks in the history of Tibetan Buddhism.

Both Kun Gongqoi Gyibo's father Sakyialhozui and his elder brother Kun Nor Xirab Cechen were pious followers of the Nyingma Sect. Kun Nor Xirab Cechen, elder brother of Kung Gongqoi Gyibo, was famous for his immense knowledge, strict observance of the Buddhist commandments, and good command of Tantric practices. He was the patriarch of the Kuns at that time, also the last master of the Kuns worshiping the Nyingma Sect. According to historical records of Tibetan Buddhism, the Kuns were divided into two periods from Kun Nor Xirab Cechen, under whom they followed the Nyingma Sect and following him they were believers in the Sagya Sect. Kun Gongqoi Gyibo followed his father and elder brother in childhood to learn the doctrines handed down from the Kuns, which belonged to the Nyingma Sect. When he grew up, however, Kun Gongqoi Gyibo began to be interested in the new Tantricism prevailing at that time in Tibetan areas. One day, he went to participate in a large-scale ceremony held in Cho, and was transported by the diverse and bustling performance, especially the magic. The magicians were attired with female characteristics, wearing goddess masks, carrying various Buddhist objects, jumping for joy and dancing gracefully. The magicians showed people a varied and colorful performance in a unique way. When Gongqoi Gyibo returned home, he told his elder brother what he had seen and asked how and why such performance could appear. His elder brother explained to him in detail. With the decline of the old Tantricism, it was a chaotic stage in the development of Buddhism. So, it was hard to become a celebrated Buddhist scholar or esoteric master of old Tantricism. As a result, the old Buddhist canons and objects they once owned, and the Three Gems of Buddhism they worshiped, should be discarded. He suggested a new Tantricism and new Buddhist system should be set up. However, when they sought to eliminate the old Tantricism, the Horse Head king and Diamond king could not be subdued owing to their

The Hall of Collecting Scriptures of the Sakgya Monastery.

The statue of Master Pgaba.

unpredictable and peerless magic. Hence, the sacred position of the two guardian deities was maintained when the Sagya Sect reconstructed the spiritual system and reselected the spiritual deities. Until today, the two guardian deities handed down from old Tantricism are enshrined by the Sagya Sect, together with alms-giving religious rituals to the sister deities of sun and moon. Followers of the Sagya Sect would throw a kind of food called Dorma to what were also known as the white guardian deities in a particular, seasonal religious ritual.

Kun Gongqoi Gyibo's elder brother advised him to approach Chomi Sakyayeshi, the great Buddhist master in T-thang at that time, and learn neo-Tantricism that was emerging in the second period of the dissemination of Tibetan Buddhism. Later, Kun Gongqoi Gyibo realized his brother's wish and created a new school for the family, that was the Sagya Sect.

Sakyayeshi, one of great translators on neo-Tantricism in the middle stages of the second period of the dissemination of Tibetan Buddhism, also known as Translator Chomi in history books, translated many significant works of neo-Tantricism and played an important role in their establishment in Tibetan Buddhism. He enjoyed an unparalleled high position especially in the history of the Sagya Sect, for he created the way to the Great Perfection, core teachings to which the Sagya Sect paid greatest attention. In a sense, the history of the Sagya is that of the development of the ways to the Great Perfection. So, apart from Master Translator Chomi, it is difficult to learn the history of the Sagya Sect, especially its teaching lineage.

Not only was Master Chomi a great translator held in high esteem throughout Tibetan areas, but also a famous teacher who cultivated many eminent monks. A great number of eminent monks once studied under his tutorship, including Gongqoi Gyibo (founder of the Sagya Sect), Master Marpa (forefather of the Gegyu Sect), Master Gui, (main spreader of the male lineage of Tantricism), the Eminent monk Soiboche (a crucial person in the formation of the

Nyingma Sect) and so on. Among of them, Gongqoi Gyibo fully succeeded and promoted Buddhist doctrines, especially the Female Lineage Bdemchogrdorje, advocated by Master Chomi.

Following his elder brother's advice, Gongqoi Gyibo began his long trek to seek Master Chomi. He encountered a master called Qin on the way and decided to learn neo-Tantricism. Gongqoi Gyibo asked Master Qin to confer on him the "Vajra initiation" and impart to him the key elements of neo-Tantricism. Unfortunately, Master Qin died under he finished his teaching. Gongqoi Gyibo had to leave for Nyegolhung Monastery, located in Lhadui of the Xigaze area, and asked to study under the tutorship of Master Chomi. At first, Gongqoi Gyibo learned Vajra neo-Tantricism under Master Chomi what Master Qin had left. In order to learn comprehensively the Great Treasure Scriptures, Gongqoi Gyibo sold part of his family lands, bought seventeen horses, together with a pear in the shape of forage grass, to present to Master Chomi as rewards for imparting Buddhism to him. Master Chomi lectured him on part of the Great Treasure Scriptures, giving priority to the Three Orders Tantricism. In addition, he especially taught the ways to the Great Perfection. Therefore, Gongqoi Gyibo came to be the most excellent successor of the teachings of Master Chomi.

In 1073, at the age of forty, Gongqoi Gyibo established a monastery at the foot of Mountain Pobori, near the bank of the Chun Qu River, namely the famous Sagya Monastery. The word "Sagya" originated from Tibetan, meaning a gray-white land, for it was built on such a land considered auspicious. From there, Gongqoi Gyibo started to impart Tantricism to disciples, mainly of the Kuns, and gradually established a new theoretical system on the lineage of neo-Tantricism. Thus, a new sect of Tibetan Buddhism came into being. Since the enclosures

A piece of fresco showing paintings of Sapan Gonggar Gyaincain and Master Pagba.

The jade seal that emperor of the Yuan Dynasty conferred to Master Pagba, State Tutor.

A villager worshiping in the Khegya Monastery in the Phunan County of the Ngari area. The Khegya Monastery, belonged to the Sakgya Sect of Tibetan Buddhism, was built in the Guge Kindom.

and most buildings of the Sagya Sect were painted with red, white and black stripes, many scholars also called it the Stripe Sect and this title began to appear in all kinds of history books. Actually, it was not a proper title.

Gongqoi Gyibo served as the Chief Abbot of the Sagya Monastery and lectured on Buddhism for nearly 30 years, laying a great foundation for the formation and development of the Sagya Sect. As far as Gongqoi Gyibo is concerned, he observed the hereditary system of the Kuns and served as a layman, not an ordained monk. So, Gongqoi Gyibo married two wives; the first wife was childless but the second wife gave birth to a son, who later became patriarch of the Sagya Sect. According to historical records, from the period of Gongqoi Gyibo, the Sagya Sect set up the tradition of hereditary handing on of the position of abbot, with the control of both politics and religion. In connection with the successive history of the Sagya Sect, it is necessary to learn some historical events of the five forefathers of the sect, who had made great contributions to the development of the Sagya Sect and were held in high esteem in the history of Tibetan Buddhism. Until today, quite a number of statues and Tangka paintings of the five are worshiped at many monasteries of other sects, apart from the Sagya Sect, which fully showed the celebrated position they held.

Gonggar Nyingbo, the first forefather of the Sagya Sect, was the only son of Gongqoi Gyibo, who was by then already elderly, and his youngest wife. In childhood, he followed his father to learn Buddhism. Unfortunately, when he was ten years old, his father passed away. At that time, the post of abbot of Sagya Monastery was temporarily held by Master Bari Renqenzha, while the main task of Gonggar Nyingbo was to learn Buddhism. Following many famous masters of India and Tibet, he extensively learned Buddhist doctrines and the teachings of the sutras and Tantras of Buddhism, including "Sutra on the Ways to the Great Perfection". His main teacher was Bari Renqenzha. In addition, Gonggar Nyingbo studied *Abhidharma-kasa* under master Zhangde Darma Nyingbo, *Madhyamika* (The

A Buddha Hall.

Middle Way) and *Hetuvidya* (Buddhist Logic) under Master Qoinrenqenzhaba and Tangmei Namche, *Collection of Tantricism* and *Black Day* under the Namkuwa Brothers, *Bdemchogrdorje* and *Bright King* under Gongtang Waimai Luozuo. It is worth special mention that he studied for four years under the tutorship of Master Xiangdun, concentrating on learning Tantras on the Ways to the Great Perfection. In addition, the great Master Bowapo from Tianzhu came to Sagya Monastery in person to impart 72 Tantricism, especially 14 profound teachings within the enclosure. So, Gonggar Nyingbo was able to obtain the comprehensive and profound Tantricism only imparted to a close disciple, becoming academically accomplished and turning into a celebrated Tantric master with great magic power. It is said that he could show six different Buddha's bodies, also regarded as the embodiment of the Goddess of Mercy.

Gonggar Nyingbo took over the post of abbot of Sagya Monastery at the age of twenty. He advocated an approach through Sutras and Tantras, especially paying attention to imparting the ways to the Great Perfection. During the 47 years he served in the post, he made great contributions to the perfection of Dharma, increasing the sect's power. So, he was respectfully called Saqin, the first forefather of the Sagya Sect. Owing to his incessant achievements, the Sagya sect developed rapidly and began to distinguish itself in Tibetan Buddhism, with great expansion of power and social influence.

Gonggar Nyingbo was a great master and at the same time he was a layman, not an ordained monk. He had four sons, successively Gonggar Ba, Soinam Chemo, Zhaba Gyaincain, and Boqen Wopo. Gonggar Ba went to India for Dharma and died aged 22 at Mogyeto; Soinam Chemo succeeded his father and became the second forefather of the Sagya Sect, followed by Zhaba Gyaincain, the third forefather of the Sagya Sect; The last son of Gonggar Nyingbo, Baiqen Wopo, unlike his elder brothers, married and fathered a family.

Soinam Chemo followed his father Ganggar Nyingbo to learn the doctrines of the Sagya Sect in childhood. When he grew up, he went to Tsangpo Monastery to study the Five Sutras by Maitreya and Hetuvidya (Buddhist Logic) under the guidance of Master Qiaque Bajisengge. He succeeded to

The deities of wild ox in the Guardian Deities' Dance in winter in the Sakgya Monastery.

the post of abbot after his father Ganggar Nyingbo died. Not long after he took over the post, Soinam Chemo handed the position to his younger brother, Zhaba Gyaincain, while he devoted himself entirely to studying Tantricism and the Sutras of Tibetan Buddhism in Tsangpo Monastery. Soinam Chemo extensively learned the Tantras and sutras, paying special attention to the practice of the esoteric sect; meanwhile, he strictly observed the commandments of Tibetan Buddhism. In addition, he was proficient in the Five Treatises of Buddhist Doctrine, namely Technology, Medicine, Grammar, Logic and Philosophy, making great contributions to promoting the further development of Tibetan traditional culture. Thus, Gonggar Nyingbo became a great scholar and eminent monk enjoying high prestige.

Zhaba Gyaincain, taking over the post from his elder brother, studied Dharma until he was twelve years old. It was said that he lectured on Hevajra Sutra so well at the age of eleven that the people around him were amazed. It was also said that he learned the Three Tantras through a dream, and fully grasped it. In addition, Zhanba Gyaincain was ordained as a upasaka (laymen) by Jamshengdawa Gyaincain, giving up wine and meat and strictly abiding by Buddhist disciplines. According to the historical record, Zhaba Gyaincain served as abbot of the Sagya Sect at the age of 13, and contributed to the growing expansion of Sagya Monastery. He ordered the construction of the Hall of Buddha on the roof of the Great Hall, and launched the project to write Gangyur of Tripitaka with gold ink. Zhaba Gyaincain put all the treasures and objects that disciples and followers offered as alms into use to erect statues of Buddhas, Buddha halls and pagodas, or helping poor farmers and herders. When he died after presiding over Sagya Monastery for 57 years, he had virtually no possessions, showing the high virtues of a monk who strictly observed religious commandments.

Gonggar Gyaincain, the youngest son of Ganggar Nyingbo, learnt Dharma from childhood to lay a solid foundation for the study of Buddhism. For instance, in childhood, he received ordination as a Upasaka (laymen) under his uncle and gained extensive Buddhist knowledge and culture. In 1204, at the age of 23, Ganggar Gyaincain went to Kashmir and studied under Master Sakya Shele. He was ordained as a Bhiksu (junior monk) under Master Sakya Shele and learned many Buddhist scriptures such as *Explanation of*

The stupa of the Beigyu Monastery, combing the construction style of the Sakgya, Bhulu, Gelug sects of Tibetan Buddhism. Its construction was started from 1414 and it took ten years to finish the construction.

Logic by Dharmakirt and *Seven Logics* including *Ornament and Clear Realization*, as well as traditional Indian and Tibetan culture such as Technology, Medicine, Grammar, Rhetoric, Words and Expressions, Syntax, Drama, Astrology and so on. As the result, in the second period of dissemination of Tibetan Buddhism, Gonggar Gyaincain was a learned scholar with good command of the Ten Treatises Buddhist Doctrine. Tibetologists divide Ten Treatises of Buddhist Doctrine into Five Treatises of Buddhist Doctrine and Five Minor Treatises of Buddhist Doctrines. The former includes Logic, Medicine, Technology, Grammar, Philosophy (including five sutras and four Tantras, the former referring to Perfection of Wisdom, the Middle Way, Monastic Discipline, Metaphysics, Logic, while the latter comprising Action Tantra, Performance Tantra, Yoga Tantra, Highest Yoga Tantra), while the latter includes Rhetoric, Words and Expressions, Syntax, Drama and Astrology. At that time, scholars proficient in the Ten Treatises of Tibetan Doctrine were respectively called Pundit, and thus Gonggar Gyaincain gained the title of Sagya Pundit, the first scholar wining such prestige throughout the Tibetan areas.

Hearing of Gonggar Gyaincain's reputation after he won the title of Sagya Pundit, Choche Garwa, together with other five Taoist scholars from south India came to Tibet and asked for a debate with him. It was held at a market near the Shengwadi Sampo Monastery of Mangyu Gyizong and lasted 13 days. Ending in failure for the Indians, who had to cut their hair and become monks. From then on, the fame of Sagya Pundit became wider known in the Tibetan areas.

As a great scholar, Sagya Pundit left rich Buddhist works and cultural commentaries, such as *Doctrine of Three Monastic Disciplines, Theory on Tibetan Logic, Introduction to Sage and Philosophy, Comments on Explanation to Instruments, Theory on Rhetoric, Theory on Grammar and Composition, Mottoes of the Sagya Sect* and so on. Among of them, *Doctrine of Three Monastic Disciplines* was an important work in which he commented on the correctness or otherwise of various views Buddhists held at that time

The statue of guardian deity of the Nanamzha Monastery in Lhindro, which was built in 1446 by the eminent monk Shanqin Rongbo of the Sakgya Sect.

The South Monastery of the Sakgya Monastery.

and elaborated his understanding and opinions of Buddhism. The book has always been a compulsory one for monks of the Sagya Sect. *Theory on Tibetan Logic* played a crucial role in Tibetan Buddhism, and was written on the basis of *Collection of Logic by Chena* and *Explanation of Logic by Dharmakirt* and added Sagya Pundit's understanding and ideological system to the existing thought. In addition, Mottoes of the Sagya Sect is a collection of oft-quoted mottoes putting more emphasis on social ethics and ways of human communications, which is quite popular with Tibetan people.

Not only was Sagya Pundit a learned Buddhist monk, but also a crucial political person who contributed much to the official incorporation of Tibet into China. Because of his high esteem in Tibetan areas, he was chosen by the ruler of the Yuan Dynasty to be a key person between the two sides. In 1264, at the invitation of Godan Khan of the Yuan Dynasty, Sagya Pundit reached Lanzhou and discussed with him the terms of Tibet's submission to Mongolia, establishing political administration of the Mongol royal court over Tibetan local forces. Sagya Pundit wrote to various local forces at Lanzhou, persuading them to accept the terms of submission. In the end, he accomplished the tasks assigned by the Yuan ruler, but he failed to return the Sagya Monastery, and died at Lanzhou at the age of 72. Sagya Pundit devoted himself to the cause of unifying his country and various nationalities. Due to his great efforts, Tibet submitted to the central administration of the Yuan Dynasty without war.

The fifth forefather of the Sagya Sect is Pagba. He was the son of Soinam Gyaincain, younger brother of Sagya Pandit. According to Song of the Cuckoo, Pagba was so quick in mind and eager to learn from childhood that he could lecture on Buddhist scriptures the age of eight. Benefiting a great deal from his uncle, Sagya Pundit, Pagba later became a celebrated political person as well as a high monk proficient in Buddhist knowledge. Pagba followed his uncle to Lanzhou for political negotiations with the Mongolian Khan when about ten years old, when he began to be exposed to a political environment, thus laying a foundation for his later political career. When he was 17, Pagba was appointed successor of the Sagya Sect by Sagya Pundit who was close to death. Pagba took over the post after his uncle died and served as abbot of Sagya Monastery and patriarch of the Sagya Sect. Pagba turned out to be an eminent person who had both religious rights in charge of Buddhist affairs of the Sagya Sect and political rights representing Tibetan local forces. Therefore, he played an important role both towards local interests in Tibet and the central government of the Yuan Dynasty. In 1253, upon the imperial edict issued by Kublai, Pagba visited him. In order to show the respect of the Yuan government, Kublai and his wives, together with their children received Pagba with full ceremony, showing themselves to be ordinary people paying homage to a great master. Altogether 25 people received Abhiseka initiation under Master Pagba, while they offered many treasures and materials in return. In 1255, Pagba went back to Tibet and reached Nyatang to pay homage to Natang Kanqin Zhaba Sanggar, under whom he was ordained as a Bhiksu, the supreme ceremony in the life of a monk. At that time, there were

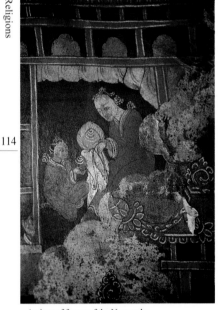

A piece of fresco of the Nanamzha Monastery in Lhindro, which was built in 1446 by the eminent monk Shanqin Rongbo of the Sakgya Sect.

frequent debates between Buddhism and Taoism thanks to Mongolian rulers' equal treatment of various religions. In 1258, In order to decide which was better, a grand debate between Buddhism and Taoism was held at the palace of Dadu (capital of the Yuan Dynasty). Menge Khan, elder brother of Kublai, ordered the latter to be responsible for the debate. Finally the Taoist side admitted failure, and 17 Taoists cut their hair to become monks, while some Taoist monasteries became Buddhist ones. When Kublai ascended to the throne as the Khan in 1260, he nominated Pagba as "State Tutor", bestowing on him a jade seal. Four years later, in 1264, Kublai Khan moved his capital to Dadu (present-day Beijing), and set up a Zhongzhi (general) Council in the central government to handle religious affairs throughout the country and administrative affairs of local Tibetan areas. Pagba was put in charge of the council in the capacity of "State Tutor". One year later, when Pagba went back to Tibet, he had the Sagya Monastery repaired and refurbished, including building new statues of Buddha, a pagoda, and writing in gold ink the Dangyur section of the Tripitaka. He followed from one master to another, studying Buddhist logic, Sutric theory, Tantric practices, as well as five treatises of Buddhist doctrine, namely traditional Tibetan culture. Many learned and accomplished masters, such as Kashmir Pundit Shidatagardabazha, Translator Lowo Xirab Reqen, Kanqenqingnamkazha from the place of Nyatang, gave him directions for his study. This time, Pagba stayed in Tibet for over three years, during which time he managed to create a set of new Mongolian characters following the order of Khan Kublai. The 41 new Mongolian characters with Mongolian pronunciation were invented according to the 30-character Tibetan alphabet. It was later called "the character of Pagba". When Pundit Pagba presented the new Mongolian characters to Kublai Khan, the king was so satisfied that he issued an imperial edict in 1268 that all editions and official documents should be written in the newly created characters, with an aim to promoting it around the country. In 1270, Pundit Pagba offered the second Vajra initiation to Kublai Khan.

A piece of fresco of the Gonggar Qoidui Monastery, which is located in Gonggar County of the Tibetan Autonomous Region. It is one of the monasteries of the Sakgya Sect of Tibetan Buddhism near Lhasa.

Due to these various actions, he was regarded highly by the Yuan ruler. As a reward for his achievements, Khan Kublai entitled Pundit Pagba as Imperial Tutor and bestowed on him jade seals accordingly. In 1276, Pagba once again reached Sagya Monastery from Dadu, this time escorted by Crown Prince Zhenjin in person. During their journey, Pundit Pagba wrote especially for and imparted to Crown Prince *Doctrines on What I Know*, which has a Chinese edition and was compiled into the Tripitaka. In 1277, at Chomirenmo near Nyatang Monastery, Pundit Pagba held a grand Dharma Gathering, also called the Chomi Gathering, in which 70, 000 Buddhist monks and followers participated. Three years later, he passed away at the early age of 46 in the Lhazhang Lhakang of Sagya Monastery. After his death, Khan Kublai conferred him respectful titles with 38 words that praised his achievements and contributions. In 1320, Emperor Renzong of the Yuan Dynasty issued an edict that temples of Imperial Tutor Pagba should be built throughout the country to commemorate this outstanding figure forever. During the time that Pagba served as State Tutor and Imperial Tutor, he made great contributions not only to the all-around development of the Tibetan areas in the terms of politics, culture and economy, but also promoting stability and development of the Yuan Dynasty as well as national unity and cultural exchanges among all the nationalities around the country. Mr. Wang Sen once stated: It seemed that Pundit Pagba, by following the internal policy of his uncle Sapan Gonggar Gyaincain, not only further consolidated the relationship of the Tibet area and the central government of the motherland, but also boosted the economic and cultural exchanges between the Han and Tibetans, as well as between the Mongolian and the Tibetan. Thereafter, it indirectly forged stronger ties among all nationalities of our country, although it was only a combination of the rulers of the Mongolian and the Tibetan. "The title of Imperial Tutor conferred by the central government of the Yuan Dynasty still continued after the death of Pagba, and the post was occupied by eminent monks of the Sagya Sect of Tibetan Buddhism. For

An old monks in the Zhigung Till Monastery.

Sorcerers' Dance of the Zhigung Till Monstery.

Tibetan Buddhism

instance, Renqin Gyaincain took the post after Pagba, then Dharma Palaregesita, the niece of Pagba, then Yeshi Renqin, and so on. Altogether over a dozen eminent monks served as Imperial Tutor until the end of the Yuan Dynasty.

Through the introduction of the five forefathers of the Sagya Sect, we can have a general knowledge of historical process of the development of the Sagya Sect in Tibetan areas. According to Tibetan historical records, the first three forefathers of the Sagya Sect were called the three white forefathers for the white ordinary clothes they wore, representing a layman identity, while the last two forefathers were known as two red forefathers, from the red robes they wore, symbolizing that they were formally Buddhist monks. There were also many grand monks who continued to play a great role in the development of Buddhism of the Sagya Sect following the five forefathers. The Four Lhazhang of the Sagya Sect were among them - namely Xitog Lhazhang, Lhakang Lhazhang, Renqingang Lhazhang, and Diqoi Lhazhang. These had been four pillars during the period when the Sagya Sect was enjoying vigorous growth, tracing their origins to the period of Master Gonggar Lobzui Gyaincain, the Imperial Tutor of China's Yuan Dynasty, whose many half-brothers presided over each Lhazhang respectively.

The Xitog Lhazhang was established when Namka Raobi Gyaincain served as abbot of the Sagya Sect. Later, when

117

Gonggar Gyaincain, the son of Mamka Raobi Gyaincain, succeeded to his father's position, he moved Xitog Lhazhang from Sagya to Qoimi. From then on, the abbot of Xitog Lhazhang was succeeded in generations by his male offspring. The last abbot was Gonggar Zhaxi Gyaincain, who was entitled State Tutor by China's Ming Dynasty. Because he had no son when he passed away, he converted the Xitog Lhazhang to the Renqengang Lhazhang. So, the Xitog Lhazhang disappeared as an independent entity.

The first abbot of the Lhakang Lhazhang was Gonggar Gyaincain Zangpo Sangpo, followed by his son, Qoigyi Gyaincain. Members of the family continued to occupy the position of abbot until its decline in the 16th century.

Renqengang Lhazhang traced its first abbot to Jamyang Dunye Gyaincain, followed in succession by Dawa Gyaincain, Jamyang Qenbo, Xeirab Gyaincain and so on. After the four generations of the Renqengang Lhazhang, some time in the 15th century, it was suspended and then disappeared.

The Diqoi Lhazhang is the direct line of descent from the Sagya Sect, which is the only one still existing. The Diqoi traced its first abbot to Gonggar Lebei Joinnei Gyanicainpo Sangbo, who served as the central government official in charge of enacting law in the Tibetan areas in the Yuan Dynasty. The abbot of the Diqoi Lhazhang was succeeded in a hereditary system from father to son. The central governments of the Yuan and Ming Dynasties paid great attention to the abbot of the Diqoi Lhazhang. For instance, Zhaba Gyaincain, the son of Gonggar Lebei Joinnei Gyaincainpo Sangbo, who was the first abbot of the Diqoi Lhazhang, was called King, while the grandson of Zhaba Gyaincain, Manke Lebe Gyaincain, was conferred the title of Assistance Religious King by Emperor Yongle of the Ming Dynasty. As the Diqoi Lhazhang is the only one with a continuous lineage until today, the abbot of the Sagya Sect was the abbot of the Diqoi Lhazhang.

In the 13th century, Tibet was officially incorporated into China. As a influential religious force at that time, the Sagya

118 The statue of Buddha Qamba worshiped in the Cemolhin Monastery.

The ugly figures of Sorcerers' Dance of the Chubo Monastery.

Sect contributed much to the unification of China and various nationalities. Henceforth, under great support of the Yuan Dynasty in both politics and economy, the Sagya Sect prospered all in Tibetan areas, becoming one of the most important sects of Tibetan Buddhism. Furthermore, for the first time, high monks from the Sagya Sect set up local forces merging politics and religion in Tibet, owing to the support and honorable titles from the central Yuan government.

Today, there are also quite a number of Sagya monasteries and disciples in Tibetan areas. Latest statistics show that altogether there are 141 Sagya monasteries in Tibetan areas, with 94 located in Tibet Autonomous Region, where its main influence remains. The Sagya Monastery, situated in Sagya County, Xigaze, is the ancestral monastery of the sect.

Historically, the Sagya Monastery comprises the Southern and Northern monasteries, but only the Southern Monastery remains today. In 1288, Benqen Sagya Sangbo built the Southern Sagya Monastery. Covering an area

The cut blocks for printing Tripitaka kept in the Cemolhin Monastery.

of 147,000 square meters, its surrounding wall is about five meters high, two meters thick, with watchtowers on each corner. The monastery boasts rich and precious religious relics and Buddhist classics, and is also known as the second Dunhuang. There are 90 monks residing in the monastery, with 11 old monks and five who have attained a degree of Rabgyamba. The institute responsible for the Sagya Sect is called the monastery management committee, composed of seven people, namely one honorary director, three deputy directors, and three committee members. It is divided into six departments, covering education, cultural relics, finance, maintenance, hygiene and reception.

With regard to teachings and religious rituals, the Sagya Monastery pays attention to both open and esoteric scriptures. One should first study theories of the open school, with two different grades of junior and senior class. The junior class, lasting six years, is a preparatory class of the Open School, during which monks study from initial classes of Tibetan Grammar, Rhetoric, Drama, Calendars and so on. In the end, they would enter the last stage to study comprehensive Buddhist scriptures, when they were required to recite six Buddhist scriptures. At present, the monastery houses 47 resident monks.

The senior class houses 15 resident monks now and its semester is also six years. They mainly studied 18 scriptures of the Sagya Sect, which are all written by eminent monks from Indian, apart from one works written by Sagya Pundit, Treasure Collection of Logic. Scholars of the Sagya Sect are always pride of the scriptures they learned, embracing that what they learned is orthodox Buddhist theory. They are qualified to participate in an examination called Rabgyamba Degree after they have finished study of the 18 Buddhist scriptures.

One may enter the esoteric school after completing the open school. He should study from theory of Tantras (scriptures of the secret school) before beginning to practice Tantricism. Then, he can receive the initiation ceremony, also called "Vessel consecration". Usually, the master pours water from a pot or vase onto the head of the disciple, and then offers him wine from a bowl made of a skull to warn him to clear his mind of all evil thoughts. After this ceremony, the monk can learn Tantricism from the master and step into

Lamas of the Zongwuer Monastery and villagers nearby.

a period of practicing meditation. They mainly practice profound meditation of Tantricism, based on "the gradual way to birth and death" and "the gradual way to the Great Perfection".

The most important religious ceremonies held in Sagya Monastery were the Ceremony of Hevajra, Worshiping Ceremony and Ceremony of Vajrapani. The Ceremony of Hevajra was held from the 8th to the 14th day of the ninth month of the Tibetan calendar. In the ceremony, the monastery held religious rituals such as reciting Buddhist scriptures, worshiping rituals, and practicing Hevajra Tantras. The worshipping ceremony, which was held from the 12th day of the eleventh month to the first day of the twelfth month of the Tibetan calendar, was a ceremony to worship spirits and deities, demons and ghosts by presenting offerings made from colorful ribbons and Tsamba (roasted highland qingke barley flour) accompanied by scripture-reciting and Dharma-dancing performed by Buddhist monks. With regard to the Ceremony of Vajrapani, it was held from the 8th day to the 18th day of the seventh month of Tibetan calendar. In the ceremony, Dharma-dancing was performed to worship Vajrapani, the principal deities of Tibetan Buddhism.

The seventh Living Buddha of the Zongwuer Monastery, also present Abbot, Tudem Targye.

In a word, the Sagya Monastery, not only is the ancestral monastery of the Sagya Sect, which enjoys high prestige among followers of the Sagya Sect, but is also a monastery of Tibetan Buddhism full of religious and cultural atmosphere famous at home and abroad.

In addition, there has another famous monastery of the Sagya Sect, the Gonggar Qoidui Monastery, which was situated in Gonggar County of the Shannan area of the Tibetan Autonomous Region. It was built in 1464 by Gudain Gonggar Namgyi, and it became an important place for the Sagya Sect to spread its doctrines of Tantricism, putting emphasis

The Buddhist scriptures, including Dangyur, Gangyur, kept in the Zongwuer Monastery.

on Tantras of the Gonggar branch. It was destroyed during the "Culture Revolution", and in 1985 the central government of People's Republic of China allocated a special fund of over 80,000 Yuan to have it repaired and renovated. Now, it has basically resumed its former look. At present, there are 14 resident monks, four old monks and the remainder rather young. The Gonggar Qoidui Monastery has established complete religious rituals and activities, such as reciting Buddhist scriptures, a ritual that all Buddhist monks of the monastery take part in. This is held in the Great Sutra Hall every morning and evening. Then, there is the Ceremony of Hevajra, held from the 9th to the 19th day of the first month in the Tibetan Calendar, and the ceremony held on the 14th day of the forth month commemorating Sapan's Parinirvana.

Besides the Tibetan Autonomous Region, there are also a number of Buddhist Monasteries of the Sagya Sect in Yushu and Ganzi Tibetan prefectures respectively in Qinghai and Sichuan provinces. Gyigu Monastery of the Yushu Tibetan Prefecture played an important role in the dissemination and development of the Sagya Sect in the area. In addition, in Yushu Tibetan Prefecture, there are also many monasteries of the Sagya Sect, such as the Reqenlun, Dongcong, and Charub monasteries in Yushu Country, Tudain and Saida monasteries in Chendo County, as well as Zongda Monastery in Qoi Village of Namchan County.

4). The Kargyu Sect

The Kargyu Sect, one of four most important sects of Tibetan Buddhism, has exerted great influence on it in the Tibetan areas. In Tibetan, "kar" means "statement of Buddha" and "gyu" means "carry forward", hence the name of "kargyu" means "handing Dharma down orally". The sect got its name as it stressed the practice of Tantricism, which was usually passed on orally from teacher to disciple. The Kargyu Sect is also known as the White Sect for the white-stripped robes that its monks always wore. This is seemingly inappropriate, just as *History and Doctrines of Different Buddhist Sects* states: "Later, some historical works from

Bhutan called it 'White Sect Lineage', which came from the tradition that Master Marpa, Master Milarapa and Master Noropa, the three forefathers of the Kargyu Sect, usually wore white robes. This style hence was handed down from generation to generation, becoming the sect's fashion. But the name of the Kargyu Sect, widely known among Tibetans, seemed to be more appropriate than that of the White Sect, because the former properly reflects its features of oral transmission of its teachings." As the book pointed out, in Tibetan "Kargyu" means "carry down orally", and it also indicates the importance of transmission of its knowledge from teacher to student, so the word "kargyu" is an appropriate one to reflect its characteristics.

The Kargyu Sect was formed "in the second period of dissemination of Tibetan Buddhism", during which it was founded by Translator and Master Marpa, who was succeeded by the Great Yogi Milarapa and Master Tabo Lhagyi. It was not until the time of Master Tabo Lhagyi that the Kargyu Sect was formally established and attained greatness, however. As is well known, among various sects of Tibetan Buddhism, the Kargyu Sect has the most numerous and jumbled branches. In terms of teaching lineage, despite its numerous and jumbled branches, there is no discernible difference on doctrines and disciplines advocated by each branch, as all can trace their origins to the lineage of Trans-

The mani stone enclosure, about 2 meters in height and 1 meter in width, of the Zongwuer Monastery.

lator and Master Marpa and Master Milarapa. Generally speaking, the sect falls into two lineage, one is called the Tabo Kargyu, founded by Translator Marpa and carried on by Master Milarapa; while the other is known as Shangpa Kargyu, created by Qoinbo Namjor. Later, the Shangpa Kargyu gradually declined and disappeared, while the Tabo Kargyu developed and flourished, developing Four Large Branches and Eight Minor Branches, as well as many other sub-branches.

The Tangka brocade kept over hundreds years in the Zongwuer Monastery in Namqu County. The Zongwuer Monastery is belonged to the Kargyu Sect.

The Shangpa Kargyu was founded by Master Qoinbo Namjor, who was born in 1085. At the age of ten, he began to study Tibetan and Sanskrit. Three years later, he started to learn the Bon religion under a great master of the Bon religion, and then changed to study "the Great Perfection" of the Nyingma Sect. When he attained certain language ability and religious knowledge, Qoinbo Namjor went to Nepal to study Sanskrit and Tantricism, taking a quantity of gold with him. Later, he traveled to India, where he received teaching from many scholars and yogis, including Master Milepa, and mastered the Vajrayana teachings popular in India at that time. When he returned to Tibet, he received monastic ordination under Master Namri Tangba, the eminent monk of the Kardam Sect of Tibetan Buddhism. Thereafter, Master Qoinbo Namjor began to build Buddhist monasteries at Phengyul, north of Lhasa, and then traveled to Shang in the Xigaze area, where he spread the Vajrayana teachings he had mastered and built many Buddhist monasteries in three years. Consequently, Shang became the foundation and center where Master Qoinbo Namjor spread his teachings and taught disciples. What's more, his influence quickly expanded around the area. The lineage he founded came to be known as the Shangpa Kargyu. It was said Master Qoinbo Namjor traveled to India to study Tantricism seven times, which indicated he gained his knowledge directly from

Indian masters rather than from the lineage of Translator Marpa. So, the disciples and followers of the Shangpa Kargyu maintained an independent lineage, even though it shared similar doctrines and rituals with the Tabo Kargyu handed down from Masters Marpa, Milarapa and Tabo Lhagyi. Anyway, the Shangpa Kargyu, compared with the Tabo Kargyu, the orthodox lineage of the Kargyu Sect, is still one of two important sects among the numerous and jumbled sects of the Kargyu Sect of Tibetan Buddhism.

The Zhigung Till Monastery in Gongkar County of Mochu. The monastery was built in 1179.

Here it is worth mentioning that Master Tongdong Gyibo, who was famous for building chain bridges in Tibet in the 15th century, was still regarded as being an eminent monk of the Shangpa Kargyu. It was said that he had built altogether over 100 chain bridges in the region, collecting money mainly by organizing people to perform Tibetan opera. Hence, he enjoyed high prestige among Tibetan people and he was worshiped in forms of statues and Tangka in many Buddhist monasteries. What's more, Many Tibetan historical works agree that many eminent Buddhist monks, including Master Tsongkapa, founder of the Gelug Sect, and his close disciple, also regarded as the first Panchan Gandain Zhuba, once studied from great scholars and translators of the Shangpa Kargyu. Therefore, the Shangpa Kargyu played an important role in the history of Tibetan Buddhism. However, from the 15th to the 16th century, it gradually declined and eventually disappeared.

While the Tabo Kargyu was the only one that not only carried on the teachings of the Kargyu Sect but has also survived until today, it was also considered as the orthodox part of the Kargyu Sect. Therefore, to some degree, the establishment of the Tabo Kargyu marked that the Kargyu Sect

The statue of Buddha, which was cast when the Zongwuer Monastery was established, is symbols of the Kargyu Sect of Tibetan Buddhism. It was made of alloy and has a history of over 500 years old.

had formally come into being.

Master Tabo Lhagyi was the founder of the Tabo Kargyu, which took his title. "Tabo" was a place in the south of the Tibet Autonomous Region, where Master Tabo Lhagyi had made great achievements in his religious cause; "Lhagyi" was a respectful title for a doctor, as Master Tabo Lhagyi started to practice medicine in his youth and gained a certain local reputation. Local people were willing to call him Tabo Lhagyi and this address spread and became his title. Master Tabo Lhagyi had many addresses, such as Master Niwa Gonggar, his born name, but was also known as Master Soinam Renqen as well as Master Gangpo Par, from the Gangpo Monastery where in his later age he used to reside and spread his teachings.

The satellite television receiver and solar equipment before the Zongwuer Monastery.

At the age of 26, he was formally ordained as a Buddhist monk. At first, he studied under Kampus Nordain and other eminent monks from Maryu Bdemchogradorje Tantricism and Vinaya (Buddhist Monastic Disciplines); then, he went to Phengyur, where he studied under Master Gyiayuwa, from whom he systematically studied the teachings handed down from Master Artisa, namely the teachings of the Kardam Sect. At that time, he achieved much in the theory of sutras and Tantras. At the same time, as he felt the importance of meditation, he built a small room near Sarka Monastery to practice meditation under the patronage of his parents. It was said that Master Tabo Lhagyi could maintain his meditation for 13 days unbroken, so as to prevent and destroy any feelings of cupidity and vexation. When he practiced, he slept little, and even after he fell asleep, he could capture the bright light of the Bodhisattva of ten states mentioned in the *Golden Bright Sutra*. He also ate nothing for five days while meditating. Through this hard way of practice, he perceived the essence of Tantricism and succeeded in attaining the great pleasure stage of Tantricism. It was not until he was 32 years old that Tabo Lhagyi heard of Master Milarapa. Then, he went to the western regions of the Tibet Autonomous Regions to seek him. On his way, he visited several formal masters of the Kardam Sect, who admonished him

The Hall of Buddha statue of the Leiwuqi Monastery in the Qamdo area, which was built in 1277 and was ancestral monastery of the Dalhung Branch of Phachu Kargyu of the Kargyu Sect.

not to throw away its teachings. After a hard trek, Tabo Lhagyi finally stood before Master Milarapa, the latter immediately perceived his marvelous ability and imparted to him all the secret teachings he owned. Master Milarapa offered Vajra initiation to Tabo Lhagyi, who practiced according to the teachings of his teacher and finally attained success. After this, he received Yoga of the Physic heat, one of six practices of Naropa. All in all, it took Tabo Lhagyi only 13 month to grasp and digest all the profound Tantricism that Master Milarapa imparted.

Thereafter, in accordance to what Master Milarapa advised and arranged, Tabo Lhagyi went back to the Lhasa area to further the practice of meditation, and three years later, he withdrew from the people and dwelled in secluded places among deep mountains and great gorges. From then on, he began to hold strong belief in the teachings of Master Milarapa, and set about the sacred ways of creating the Tabo Kargyu School of the Kargyu Sect. In 1121, at Talha Gangpo, on the north bank of the Yarlung Zangbo River in today's Tabo area, the master built a monastery (Gangpo Monastery). This became the base from which Master Tabo Lhagyi set out to impart the teachings he had grasped and perceived, cultivating a large number of disciples. His famous work Gradual Ways to Deliverance, written on the basis of *Gradual Ways to Enlightenment of the Kardam Sect* and *Great Scale*

A piece of Tangka in the Dalhung Monastery of Lhinzhou County in the Qamdo area.

The statue of Sakyamuni in the Dalhung Monastery of Lhindro County, which was built in 1180. It belonged to the Dalhung Branch of Phachu Kargyu of the Kargyu Sect.

Teachings by Milarapa, was one of the compulsory courses of Tabo Kargyu. So, it is reasonable that many scholars of later ages held that the Tabo Kargyu merged the teachings of the Kardam into Kargyu sects, one of its characteristics.

Master Tabo Lhagyi presided over the religious affairs of the Gangpo Monastery for over 30 years, until, in 1150, he resigned his position in favor of his niece, Gongba Cechen Nyingbo, who was also the main successor of the Tabo Kargyu. Thereafter, the Abbot of the Gangpo Monastery was always one of descendents of Master Tabo Lhagyi, whose family continued to live and reside there. It is known that after the demise of Gongba Cechen Nyingbo, the Abbot of the Gangpo Monastery succeeded according to the system of Reincarnation of the Living Buddha, so the Tabo Kargyu was regarded as one of several sects taking the lead in developing this system in the Tibetan areas. Gangpo was famous for Master Tabo Lhagyi, but in the end it failed to form a large-scale monastery. However, the greatest contribution he made was that he cultivated four close disciples who then built monasteries and spread Buddhism in the Lhasa and Xigaze areas. Thus, there came into being four comparatively independent branches of the Tabo Kargyu - namely, the Karma, Phachu, Bharong and Chaipa Branches -- that marked that the Tabo Kargyu, or the Kargyu Sect in a wider

The outer view of the Dalhung Monastery of Lhindro County.

sense, beginning to enter its prime period of flourishing.

(1). The Karma Branch of the Tabo Kargyu

The Karma Branch is the most influential sect of the Kargyu Sect of Tibetan Buddhism, and it was also the first sect to adopt the Reincarnation System of Living Buddha. What's more, the Karma Branch established in succession several reincarnation systems of Living Buddha, among of which the Black Cap lineage and the Red Cap lineage were the most famous. Thereafter, the Karma Branch was of great importance in Tibetan Buddhism.

It was founded by Master Dusun Qenba, one of four famous disciples of Master Tabo Lhagyi. He was born at Dorkangzhexuegang Gyirewa, and his family was of the clan of Tadong Garpo. His father, Gongba Dorjegongbo, was a Tantric yogi. At the age of eleven, Dusun Qenba followed his father to learn Buddhist prayers and simple practices of Tantricism. Five years later, he was ordained as a Buddhist monk and was given the ordination name Qoigyi Zhaba by Kampus Cholha Chesengezha of Qoigo Monastery. At the age of 19, he left for the Lhasa area to study Buddhism. At first, he systematically studied under Master Duilhung Gyiamawa and Master Kaba Qoigyisengge *Five Sutras by Maitreya*, *The Middle Way*, *Buddhist Logic* and other basic Buddhist theories, then he went to Master Shiareba and other eminent monks, from whom he studied *Gradual Ways to Enlightenment* and other teachings of the Kardam Sect. He also received ordination from Kampus Meiduseng, who taught him Buddhist monastic disciplines. Dusun Qenba moved from one master to another, and in this way he systematically studied comprehensive sutras and Tantras. When he was aged 30, he succeeded in paying a visit to Great Master Tabo Lhagyi, under whom he studied for about three years, and grasped the essence of Tantricism of the Kargyu Sect, especially learning the practice of meditation, in which he attained the best achievements. From then on, he rose to become an erudite master of Tibetan Buddhism and shouldered responsibility for promoting the Tabo Kargyu. After he re-

A piece of Tangka in the Dalhung Monastery of Lhindro County.

The statues of eight main disciples of Buddha Sakyamuni in the Dalhung Monastery of Lhindro County. The monastery belonged to the Dalhung Branch of Phachu Kargyu of the Kargyu Sect.

turned home in 1157, at Karma near Dorkhang Changdu Leiwuqi, Master Dusun Qenba established the Karma Lhading Monastery, also known as the Karma Dansa Monastery. From this base, he tried his best to propagate the teachings of the Kargyu Sect as well as his own teachings. Thus, there came into being the Karma Branch, named after the Karma Lhading Monastery, the first to divide from the Tabo Kargyu. At that time, at Dorkhang, there were altogether over one thousand disciples who followed Master Dusun Qenba, who controlled certain social powers in the area. He exerted great influence on the development of the Karma Branch of Tabo Kargyu, especially in the political and social situation of the Tibet Autonomous Region. For instance, he often mediated in large and important local conflicts, donated large quantities of treasures to the Gangpo Monastery and other monasteries in the Lhasa areas. In his later years, he went back the Lhasa area, and in 1189, he built Chubo Monastery at nearby Duilhung. Thereafter, the Karma Lhading and Duilhung monasteries became two ancestral monasteries of the Karma Branch of the Kargyu Sect of Tibetan Buddhism, while the Chubo Monastery was reconstructed many times and turned out to be the chief monastery of the Karma Branch of the Kargyu Sect.

Master Dusun Qenba died at the age of 83 at the Chubu Monastery he had established, but, before dying, he left an injunction that he would reincarnate, so his reincarnated soul boy should be searched for after his death. It was the great invention of Master Dusun Qenba, pioneering the "Reincarnation System of Living Buddhas" in the history of Tibetan Buddhism and even the whole of Buddhism.

The direct lineage of the Living Buddha system of the Karma Branch of Tabo Kargyu that Master Dusung Qenba created was the Living Buddha later called the "Black Cap Lineage" and also the Abbot of Chubo Monastery. With regard to the title of the Living Buddha of the Karma Kargyu and its origins, History and Doctrines of Different Buddhist Sects has the answer: "Although it was said that Master Dusun Qenba wore a black cap, so that the lineage he

The Great Sutra Hall of the Leiwuqi Monastery in the Qamdo area, which was built in 1277 as the ancestral monastery of the Dalhung Branch of Phachu Kargyu of the Kargyu Sect.

The Butter Lamp Festival of Lhasa held in the fifth day of the first month of Tibetan calendar.

created was called 'the Black Cap Lineage', in fact it was from Master Karma Bashi that the lineage gained the title of 'Black Cap Lineage'. The emperor granted Master Karma Bashi a black cap symbolizing his official position." Concerning the accounts that Master Dusung Qenba wore the black cap, legend states: "At that time, hundreds of flying Taras weaved a special cap with their hairs and presented it to Master Dusung Qenba, and from then on [he] often wore this special and marvelous black cap." Actually, it is only an imaginary story and the historical record shows it was the second Living Buddha Karma Bashi who attained a black cap. The Black Cap Lineage was named after a black cap with gold edges that the Mongolian Khan Meng Ge bestowed on Master Dusung Qenba. Afterwards, it was handed down to the 17th lineage. Meanwhile, the Red Cap Lineage was named after a red cap with golden edges conferred by the Yuan government. When it was handed down to the 10th lineage, the Qing government banned the Red Cap Lineage because it was accused of involvement in a Gurkha invasion of the Xigaze area. From then on, the lineage of the Red Cap was ended.

Generally speaking, the history of the Karma Branch of the Tabo Kargyu was developed with the two main threads, the Black Cap Lineage and the Red Cap Lineage. So from the course of the two lineages' origination, development, and declination, we can acquire the whole history and current situation of the Karma Branch of the Tabo Kargyu.

(2). The Chaipa Branch of the Tabo Kargyu

The Chaipa Branch was one of four branches of the Tabo Kargyu. It was founded by Master Chaipa Zunchuzha, the second-generation disciple of Master Tabo Lhagyi. He was born in Chapazhu near Lhasa, and his father was a layman who primarily practiced Tantricism. Under his family's daily influence, Chaipa Zunchuzha began to learn Buddhism from childhood: he learned Tibetan at the age of seven, practiced Tantricism at the age of nine, and then went to Shekhang for further study. At the age of 26, he was ordained as a Bhiksu and received the ordination name of Zunchuzha. In 1153, he got an opportunity to visit Master Cechen Nyingbo, the niece of Master Tabo Lhagyi, from whom he studied the sutras and Tantras of the Tabo Kargyu. In 1175, with the financial support of Feudal Lord Garer Gyiaweiqoinei from Chaigongtang near Lhasa, Chaipa Zunchuzha built the Chaipa Monastery at Chaishika, and thus formed the Chaipa Branch of the Tabo Kargyu. In 1187, they built the Chaigongtang Monastery nearby. From then on, as the two main foundations of the Chaipa Branch, the Chaipa and Chaigongtang monasteries played an important role in its further development and extended influence. In 1268, the Abbot of the Chaipa Monastery Sanggyi Ozhu was installed as Abbot of Chaipa Myriarchiey, and thus the Chaipa Branch of the Tabo Kargyu came into being as one of the important local sect powers in the Lhasa area. As some Tibetologists have said: "The politico-religion organization of the Chaipa Branch of the Tabo Kargyu meant religion at first assisted politics, and then became a substitute for it. In the end, the Garer family wholly controlled all the politico-religious powers. That is to say, religious power became a component of their political power. It was a special form of the politico-religious system in the U-Tsang areas." (Wujun: Discrimination and Analysis on the Question of Tibetan Religion) The politico-religious powers of Chaipa once united the

A foreign tourist helping lama who will perform Sorcerers' Dance to put up a awning.

Sakya Sect and other local powers of Tibetan Buddhism to create the competing Phayzhu Branch of the Tabo Kargyu, but they were defeated in the end. Thereafter, the Chaipa Branch of the Tabo Kargyu went into decline. Later, with the flourishing of the Gelug Sect, the Chaipa and Chaigongtang monasteries were annexed and forced to become monasteries of the Gelug Sect, leading to the end of the Chaipa Branch of the Tabo Kargyu.

(3). The Bharong Branch of the Tabo Kargyu

The Bharong Kargyu was founded by Master Darma Wanggyiu (living in the middle of the 12th century), who was one of the close disciples of Master Tabo Lhagyi. Master Darma Wanggyiu built the Bharong Monastery at Angren near Xigaze. From this base, Master Darma Wanggyiu lectured on doctrine and taught disciples, and thus came into being the Bharong Branch of the Tabo Kargyu. Master Darma Wanggyiu mainly imparted the Great Scale Way of Tantricism and the Great Scale Stage of Sutraism and formed his own lineage. When he passed away, the chief abbot of the Bharong Monastery was chosen in a hereditary system among his descendents. However, the Bharong Branch came to be divided and declined due to continuous family disputes.

(4). The Phachu Branch of the Tabo Kargyu

The beast-shaped decoration on the gold roof of the Potala Palace.

The Gandain Monastery of the Gelug Sect of Tibetan Buddhism.

Lamas participating in religious ceremony held once every year in the Tashilhungbo Monastery.

The Phachu Branch is the largest among the four branches of the Tabo Kargyu. Its founder was Phamo Chupa (1110-1170), one of famous disciples of Master Tabao Lhagyi. He was born at Zhilhung Namshei in the southern area of Shekhang. In his childhood, Phamo Chupa began to study Buddhist scriptures under many teachers, and at the age of nine, he became a Buddhist monk and was named Dorgye Gyalpo. When he was 19, he happened to be an attendant of a rich man who journeyed to study Buddhism, giving Phamo Chupa an opportunity to study the teachings of various sects such as the Nyingma, Kardam and Sakya sects and so on. Later, Phamo Chupa paid a visit to Master Tabo Lhagyi, under whom he studied the teachings of the Tabo Kargyu and rose to be one of the most famous disciples of Master Tabo Lhagyi. He later went back his homeland of Shekhang, where he accepted many disciples and imparted the Tantricism mainly got from Master Tabo Lhagyi and other teachings. Master Phamo Chupa was famous for his particular teachings and his reputation spread quickly in the neighborhood. In 1158, he left his homeland for the Tibet Autonomous Region and built a small monastery at Phamo, later well known as the Dansa Till Monastery. The construction of the Dansa Till Monastery marked the formal establishment of the Phachu Branch of the Tabo Kargyu. Master Phamo Chupa resided and lectured on the teachings of the Phachu Branch at Dansa Till Monastery for 13 years, and attained Parinirvana at the age of 60. In 1351, at Zedam in the Shannan area, Master Jamgqu Cyaincain built another monastery of the Phachu Branch, namely the Zedam Monastery. The Dansa Till and Zedam monasteries stressed different contents: the former stressed the practices of meditation of Tantricism, while the latter put emphasis on imparting Buddhist Sutra Theory. It deserves noting that the Phachu Branch of the Tabo Kargyu had a close relationship with politics: It set up with the clan of the Lhang family a local power base merging politics and religion to control the U-Tsang area for over 130 years until 1481, when it was overthrown by his subordinate Renbangba. Generally speaking, the Phachu Branch of the Tabo Kargyu was famous for the high virtues that its monks possessed, such as thrift, observing strict commandments, and the deep knowledge they attained. Therefore, altogether as many as 800 Buddhist monks and disciples assembled at the Dansa Till Monastery at one time, among of which there were over ten celebrated figures. Those eminent monks respectively managed to build monasteries and advocated their teachings in the Tibetan areas, and thus came into being the eight minor branches of the Phachu Branch of the Tabo Kargyu.

Four Major Branches and Eight Minor Branches of the Kargyu Sect

The sandalwood carving of Buddha Sakyamuni and 18 Arhats worshiped at Neidui Lhakang of the Sera Monastery of the Gelug Sect. It was given in 1416 by Emperor Chengzu of China's Ming Dynasty as a present to Sagya Yeshes, one of disciples of Master Zongkapa, the founder of the Gelug Sect.

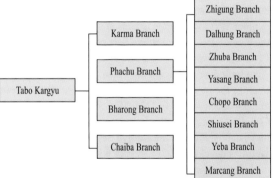

Tabo Kargyu	Karma Branch	Zhigung Branch
	Phachu Branch	Dalhung Branch
		Zhuba Branch
		Yasang Branch
	Bharong Branch	Chopo Branch
		Shiusei Branch
	Chaiba Branch	Yeba Branch
		Marcang Branch

The Living Buddha Phabalha Geleinamgyi, deputy chairman of the Standing Committee of the National People's Congress, presiding in the Qambalhin Monastery over the regular religious activities, such as reciting Buddhist scriptures and so on.

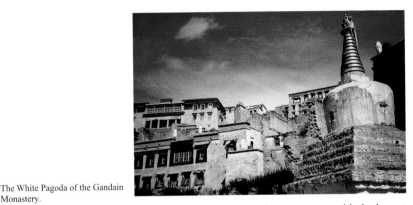

The White Pagoda of the Gandain Monastery.

The Kargyu Sect, as an important sect with the largest number of branches of Tibetan Buddhism, had quite a large number of Buddhist monasteries and disciples. At present, the monasteries of the Kargyu Sect cover the Tibetan areas. From the viewpoint of time, the monasteries of the Kargyu were built over 300 years later than those of the Nyingma Sect, as the monasteries of the former were built with its gradual development. In 1121, Master Tabo Lhagyi built the Gangpo Monastery, ushering in the new period of the formal establishment of the Kargyu Sect. Thereafter, with its vigorous development, especially with the continual emergence of its branches, the monasteries of the Kargyu Sect covered all of the Tibetan areas -- the Tibet Autonomous Region and the Tibetan areas of Qinghai, Sichuan, Gansu and Yunnan provinces. According to latest statistics, in the Tibetan areas there are altogether 366 monasteries of the Kargyu Sect, which was the third after the Gelug and Nyingma sects in terms of number of monasteries. With regard to its distribution, the Tibet Autonomous Region ranks first with 217 monasteries, followed by Qinghai Province, with 101 monasteries, then Sichuan and Yunnan provinces, respectively with 43 and five monasteries.

We have learned the distribution of the monasteries of the Kargyu Sect in the Tibetan areas of People's Republic of China. As far as the internal parts of various areas are concerned, the monasteries of the Kargyu Sect are distrib-

Unfolding Buddha painting in the Gandain Monastery.

uted unevenly. For instance, the Tibet Autonomous Region possesses 277 monasteries of the Kargyu Sect, the largest number of those in Tibetan areas. But in regard to their distribution, those monasteries stand far apart from one another. Their distribution is: 23 monasteries in Lhasa, 20 in Nyingchi, 39 in Shannan, 29 in Xigaze, 14 in Ngari, 28 in Nagou, and 78 in Qamdo. We can see the Qamdo area and the Tibet Autonomous Region have the largest number of monasteries. But compared with Yushu Prefecture of Qinghai Province, the Qamdo area is only ranked second in terms of the monasteries of the Kargyu Sect. This is because, among the 101 monasteries of the Kargyu Sect in Qinghai Province, there are as many as 93 in the Yushu area. In terms of geographical location, the Qamdo area in the Tibet Autonomous Region and the Yushu area in Qinghai Province border on each other, comprising comparative large influential circles of the Kargyu Sect. So, it is obvious that the two areas possess the largest number of disciples and the strongest influence.

The statue of Buddha Qamba in the Tashilhungbo Monastery of the Xigaze area, the largest bronze statue of Buddha throughout country, with a height of 26.7 meters.

In addition, viewed from the internal power of different branches of the Kargyu Sect, the Karma Branch of the Tabo Kargyu covers most of the Tibetan areas and each area has many Buddhist monasteries. For instance, in the Tibetan areas of Yunnan Province, which is far away from the Tibet Autonomous Region, there are three Buddhist monasteries of the Karma Branch out of five monasteries of the Kargyu Sect. It is obvious that the Karma Branch of the Tabo Kargyu has exerted a certain influence on the Tibetan areas.

Besides the Karma Branch, the Zhigung Branch also possesses comparatively great influence on the Tibetan areas. Around 1179, Master Renqenbei, the founder of the Zhigung Sub-Branch of the Phachu Branch, established its first monastery at Zhigung, the Zhigung Till Monastery, and thus the name of the sect came into being. The monastery stands today on the rise and fall of the Zhigung Sub-Branch of the Phachu Branch. Therefore, the Zhigung Till Monastery, as the ancestral monastery or the originating place of the Zhigung Sub-branch, has played a leading role in its

The overview of the Zhaibung Monastery of the Gelug Sect.

The Gangyur of Tripitaka in Tibetan edition, written by the 13th Dalai Lama in gold ink, which was kept in the Zhaibung Monastery in Lhasa.

continuation. Zhigung Till Monastery, located in today's Mochugongka County of the Tibet Autonomous Region, has 92 resident Buddhist monks, which is rare among all monasteries of the Zhigung Sub-Branch. So, it still maintains quite a large scale today, maintaining its prestige as the ancestral monastery among all the monasteries of the Zhigung Sub-Branch. It deserves mention that there are quite a number of Buddhist nunneries in the monasteries of the Zhigung Sub-Branch. There are five or six nunneries among the 21 Buddhist monasteries in the Yushu Tibetan Autonomous Prefecture in Qinghai Province, and quite a number of nuns reside in them. Today, there are 80 nuns in the Tarma Monastery in Namchan County of the Yushu area of Qinghai Province, 76 nuns in the Meiqin Monastery and 60 nuns in the Gaimar Monastery. So, it is obvious that the Zhigung Sub-Branch still maintains great influence in the Tibetan areas.

In terms of the position and its influence, the Dalhung Sub-branch has many similarities to the Zhigung Sub-branch. Dalhung Monastery, which was founded in 1180 by Master Dalhung Tangba Zhashibei, was the ancestral monastery of

Followers of Tibetan Buddhism paying homage to the Sera Monastery.

the Dalhung Sub-branch, playing an important role in its development and being held high regard in Tibetan Buddhism. It once made its way to part of the Tibetan areas of Gansu Province. For instance, in the northeast of Tianzhu Town of Gansu Province, there was a monastery with the same name. Historical records show that the Dalhung Monastery in Gansu Province was built by a Buddhist monk of the Dhalhung Lineage of the Kargyu Sect of Tibet Buddhism. However, the monastery was later converted to the Gelug Sect. At present, the Dalhung Monastery, located at Lingzhou County of the Tibet Autonomous Region, has basically resumed its former scale, with 105 resident monks. So, whether in terms of construction scale or social influence, it qualifies as a middle-level monastery.

The outer view of the Hall of Zhashinamgyi on the east of Panchen Hall in the Tashilhungbo Monastery.

The Zhuba Sub-branch also has many monasteries in the Tibetan areas of the People's Republic of China. For instance, there are 10 monasteries of the Zhuba Sub-Branch in the Yushu Tibet Autonomous Prefecture in Qinghai Province, and among of them are several large-scale ones, including the Sanmei Monastery in Namqian County, with over 250 resident monks; the Chaichiu Monastery (over 270). In addition, there are also several middle-scale Buddhist nunneries of the Zhuba Sub-Branch in the Yushu Tibet Autonomous Prefecture. The ancestral monastery of the Zhuba Sub-Branch, the Relhung Monastery, has resumed its original look. Although a small-scale monastery, it is of crucial importance to the Zhuba Sub-branch of the Phachu Branch of the Tabo Kargyu. It stands on a summer pasture with an elevation of over 4,000 kilometers, at Relhung Village of Jamchi County in the Xigaze area of the Tibet Autonomous Region. Apart from the beautiful scenery and cool weather in the brief summer, it is bitterly cold in the other three seasons. Due to this, worshipers are fewer in number compared to other monasteries. Therefore, every hall in the monastery is usually locked except in summer. However, as the ancestral monastery, the Relhung Monastery not only maintains its important position among the monasteries of the Zhuba Sub-branch around the country, but also holds high prestige abroad. At present, there are 20 resident monks. The Zhuba Sub-branch has made its way into Bhutan, Sikkim and other foreign countries, and sometimes the Relhung Monastery receives financial support from its foreign monasteries.

As far as the situation and influence of all the monasteries of the Kargyu Sect, there are three deserving special mention, which are the Chubu Monastery in Lhasa, Leiwuqi Monastery in the Qamdo area and Babung Monastery in the Ganzi area of Sichuan Province. These three monasteries have their own features and advantages. The Chubu Monastery, located in Duilhungdeqing County of Lhasa, as the ancestral monastery of the Karma Branch of the Tabo Kargyu, has a long history and was the formal residence of Living Buddha Karmaba of the Black Cap Lineage of the Kargyu Sect. Despite its limited number of resident monks, small scale and simple construction style, the Chubu Monastery still holds high prestige.

The Leiwuqi Monastery was built in 1276. Located in Leiwuqi County of Qamdo, the monastery was famous for it large scale and grand construction. In its heyday, there were over 4,000 resident monks, which was seldom seen in other Tibetan monasteries and only a few monasteries of the Gelug Sect, such as Zhaibung and Sera monasteries, can compare. From that we can learn the degree to which the Leiwuqi Monastery flourished. With regard to which sect it belongs

A part of the Tar Monastery.

to, some say the Karma Branch of the Tabo 'Kargyu, but it actually belongs to the Dalhung Sub-branch of the Phachu Branch of the Tabo Kargyu. At present, the Leiwuqi Monastery is still a large-scale monastery in the Tibetan areas, housing over 400 resident monks, which in the Tibet Autonomous Region ranks third after Tashilhungpo Monastery in the Xigaze area and Zhaibung Monastery in the western suburbs of Lhasa. So it can be concluded that the Leiwuqi Monastery is the largest monastery in scale of the Kargyu Sect in the Tibetan areas of People's Republic of China.

The construction groups of the Labrang Monastery.

Babung Monastery, situated in Dege County of Ganzi Tibetan Autonomous Prefecture of Sichuan Province, is the largest monastery in terms of scale and influence in this area. The monastery was built in 1727, and, although its history is not very long, it developed rapidly due to the support of Tusi Dege, and possesses many sub-monasteries in the neighborhood. In 1957, it housed over 500 resident monks and possessed 70-80 sub-monasteries. At present, Babung Monastery still maintains its influence. In Yushu Prefecture of Qinghai Province, where there are quite a number of sub-monasteries.

In terms of the situation of its monasteries and its influence in the entire Tibetan area, the Kargyu Sect ranks third after the Gelug and Nyingma sects. Viewed from the course of historical development, the influence of the Kargyu Sect eventually declined in the Tibetan areas. Especially in the late Ming and early Qing dynasties, with the formation and increasing expansion of the Gelug Sect, its influence declined rapidly. The reason is that the Gelug Sect adopted a measure to merge or convert the monasteries of the Kargyu Sect, thus causing the latter to gradually lose influence.

5). The Gyonam Sect

The Gyonam Sect, as with other sects of Tibetan Buddhism, has its characteristic doctrines that have aroused disputes over history. Its main theory is called "Views of the Other Void", and it traces its origins back to Master Yumo Migyodorje (around the early stage of 12th century). At first,

In 1998, the seven-year-old Living Buddha Qoinbo Arwangqamb Gyaincain, together with his sutra teacher, watching the performance of Sorceres' Dance on the Siqinmogye Rostrum of the Tashilhungbo Monastery.

The Pattra-leaf Sutra kept at the Gandain Lhakang of the Zhaibung Monastery in Lhasa.

he was a yogic layman, later being ordained as a Buddhist monk and taking the ordainment name of Dambagyibo. He studied profound Tantricism under Kashmiri Master Banqen Dawagongbo, Zotun Namlhachi, one of disciples of Master Banqen Dawagongbo, and many other eminent Buddhist monks. When the teachings of the "Views of the Other Void" were handed down to Master Gongbang Tegyitsunzhu, the fifth disciple of Master Yumo Migyodorje, the Gyonam Sect came into being. At that time, Master Gongbang Tegyitsunzhu built Gyonam Monastery at Gyomonam in the northeast of Lhachi in the Xigaze area, and the Gyonam Sect began its religious activities. He had a talented disciple, Katsun Yundam Gyaincain, who succeeded to the lineage of the Gyonam Sect and took great pains to cultivate his successor, namely Master Dorpuba Xirab Gyaincain, the sect's eminent monk. The sect further developed during the time of Master Dorpuba Xirab Gyaincain. Thereafter it went into temporary decline, but revived thanks to some celebrated figures, such as Master Gyonam Gonggar Choqoi, Master Gyonamwa Tolonamta and so on. Among them Master Gyonamwa Tolonamta made an especial contribution.

Also called Gonggar Nyingbo, he was born at Kareqoinzeng on the border of the Lhasa and Xigaze areas. It was said that he was the reincarnated soul of Master

Gonggar Choqoi. In his childhood, Tolonamta studied Buddhist scriptures in Gyonam Monastery. Later, he went from one teacher to another throughout the Tibetan areas to study Buddhist sutras and Tantras. At the age of 30, he was ordained as a Bhiksu and became an eminent monk of the Gyonam Sect. At first, the leadership in Lhaduijam supported his cause, but in the 16th century, this local power went into decline. Fortunately, Disi Zangbahan, the leader of another local power, came to his aid. So, in 1614, Master Tolonamta built another middle-scale monastery near Gyonam Monastery, namely Tadanpencholhin Monastery. From then on, Gyonam Monastery began to flourish once again. Not long after it was built, Master Tolonamta, at the invitation of the Khan of Outer Mongolia, went to the north of the Gobi desert (today's Ulan Bator) and stayed there for over 20 years to propagate Buddhism. Master Tolonamta managed to build many monasteries there, where the Kara Tribe worshipped. Because of his great efforts, Master Tolonamta was respectfully called Jebtsundamba and enjoyed high prestige in the Khulun area. In 1634, he achieved Parinirvana at Khulun. In the following year, Khan Tusheitu of the Karka Tribe happened to have a son, and the boy was regarded as the reincarnated soul of Master Tolonamta, so that the first Jebtsundamba appeared.

The huge bronze statue of Buddha Qamba kept in the hall on the third floor of the Zhaibung Monastery, which was highly worshiped by masses of followers.

In 1649, he traveled to Tibet to study Buddhism. When he finished his study and was to return home, the 5th Dalai Lama, relying on his religious powers, ordered Jebtsundamba to convert to the Gelug Sect, thus leading the masses of the outer Mongolian area to follow the Gelug way. What's more, the 5th Dalai Lama converted all the monasteries of the Gyonam Sect, including the famous Tadanpencholhin Monastery to the Gelug Sect. Only History of Indian Buddhism by Tolonamta and other occasional works of the Gyonam

The Stupa of the tenth Panchen of the Tashilhungbo Monastery.

Sect were left, while other scriptures advocating its teachings were burnt or hidden away. Therefore, by the end of the 17th century, the Gyonam Sect had disappeared in the Tibet Autonomous Region, but it succeeded in surviving in other Tibetan areas. At present, the Gyonam Sect still maintains certain influence in the Arbei area of Sichuan Province and the Golo Area of Qinghai Province. For instance, there are altogether over 30 of its monasteries in Arba, Markhang, Rangtang counties in the Arba Prefecture, and in Gande, Juchi, Banma counties of Golo Prefecture. Among them, Namtang Monastery in Namtang County, as the ancestral monastery of the Gyonam Sect in the Arba and Golo areas, still enjoys high prestige and position among disciples and followers of the Gyonam Sect.

At present, in Namtang County, there are seven main monasteries, namely Shayan, Hungtub, Risob, Gayatang, Qutang, Zhongnamtang, and Gongbolhagang. In Markhang County, there are Hermoya, Ganmonoi, Barlhang, Khangshan, Yanmodi, Zhaxirigang and Ranggu monasteries and others. In Arba County there are mainly the Segongbar, Cinam, Tarjo, Yagung and Arho monasteries.

In Gande County of the Golo Tibetan Autonomous Prefecture of Qinghai Province, there are three main monasteries. They are: Zhaxiqulhang Monastery, with 70 resident monks; Lhungshigyi Monastery, with over 70 resident monks; Chayilhung Monastery, with 25 resident monks. When Chayilhung Monastery holds religious activities, over 145 Buddhist monks usually assemble there.

In Banma County of the Golo Tibetan Autonomous Prefecture, there are primarily Arshijamgyigung Monastery, with 48 resident monks and two living Buddhas, as well as Namben Monastery, with 46 resident monks.

In Juchi County of the Golo Tibetan Autonomous Prefecture, there are primarily two monasteries. They are: Jammo Monastery, which housed 100 resident monks in the monastery and over 200 floating monks in society; as well as Nyingchi Monastery, with 65 resident monks. In fact, Nyingchi Monastery was a particular monastery that combined to follow the Gelug Sect and the Gyonam Sect, and always monks of two sects presided over religious activities.

(6). The Gelug Sect of Tibetan Buddhism

Started from Tsongkapa, the Gelug Sect was one of the last important ones to form. Tsongkapa is an eminent person in Tibetan history, not only as the founder of the Gelug Sect, but also as a philosopher and religious reformer.

He was born in the Zongka area of Amdo, around today's Tar Monastery in Hongzong County of Qinghai Province. Later, he was honored with the title of Master Tsongkapa. At the age of seven, he formally became a monk under Master Tunzurenqin at Shaqoin Monastery, which was located in eastern Qinghai province, north of the Yellow River. From then on, he got his ordination name Lobsam Zhaba. After ten years of hard work, he attained a substantial grasp of Buddhist classics from both the open and secret schools. In 1372, when he was 16, he left for the U-Tsang region to study Buddhist scriptures. In 1374, he reached Lhasa and began his career for the study of Buddhism. He followed many grand masters of different sects such as the Nyingma, Kargyu, Sakya, and Kardam sects. In the end, he gradually formed his own religious ideology combining features of other sects. In 1402, on the basis of the famous Buddhist scripture *The lamp that Shows the Path to Enlightenment*,

The inner view Purdain Lhakang of the Shalhu Monastery, in which Master Purdain, flanked by his disciples, was worshiped in the monastery.

written by Master Artisa, he finished *The Gradual Way to Enlightenment*, and then, in 1406, *The Gradual way to Tantricism*, a work about esoteric school of Tibetan Buddhism. Both works represent his ideology.

In 1409, under the financial support of Renqinbei and his son Renqinlhungbo, local nobles in Phachu, Tsongkapa constructed the Gandain Monastery along the slopes of Wangbori Mountain, 30 kilometers northeast of Lhasa. After that, Tsongkapa established a complete monastic institution as well as monk-education system. He required his disciples to strictly abide by Buddhist disciplines, give equal importance to the open and esoteric schools and follow the priority order of learning scriptures, namely open school sutras before esoteric school Tantras. Henceforth, another new sect of Tibetan Buddhism, based on Gandain Monastery, began to form, putting a perfect end to formation of various sects of Tibetan Buddhism. In 1416, Tsongkapa ordered Jamyang Qoigyi, one of his disciples, to build Zhaibung Monastery in the western suburbs of Lhasa, and in 1418, another monastery called Sera monastery in the northern suburbs of Lhasa by Sagya Yeshe, also Tsongkapa's disciple, Thus, the three main monasteries of Lhasa had been formed, which laid a foundation for the development of the Gelug sect.

Following the construction of the three monasteries in Lhasa, in 1447, the Tashilhungpo Monastery was built by Gandain Zhuba (1391-1474), one of disciples of Master Tsongkapa, in the Xigaze area. Later, Shashirabsambo built the Qamdo Monastery in the Qamdo area, and Shashirabsambo constructed Damo Monastery in the Ali area of western Tibet. Thus, the Gelug Sect had developed a comparatively solid monastic organization throughout the Tibetan areas. Its influence spread rapidly and soon surpassed its predecessors, which was unprecedented in the history of Tibetan Buddhism. In the 16th century, its initial scale had come into being in the Tibetan areas, and then in 1642, the Gelug sect gained its political leading position and posed a threat to other sects, owing to the Fifth Dalai Lama's author-

The Sutra Hall of the Qambalhin Monastery in the Qamdo area of the Tibetan Autonomous Region, where lamas often recite Buddhist scriptures.

ity who had gained titles and support from the central government of the Qing dynasty. Many monasteries of other sects was forced to convert to the Gelug Sect. Its six monasteries (namely Gandain, Sera, Zhaibung monasteries of Lhasa, Tar and Tashilhungbo Monasteries respectively in today's Qinghai and Gansu provinces, and Labrang Monastery in Gansu Province), and its

A Mosque in Lhasa.

four Living Buddha system (namely Dalai, Panchen, Zhamgya, and Jebtsundamba) are symbols of the authority and power of the Gelug Sect, which has had profound influence on people's lives in the fields of politics, economy and culture among the Tibetan, Mongolian and other nationalities. The following is a brief introduction of the present situation.

(1). Gandain Monastery

Gandain Monastery, as one of the six key monasteries of the Gelug Sect and three major monasteries located in Lhasa, is the ancestral monastery of the Gelug Sect. Built along the slopes of Wangbori Mountain about 30 kilometers northeast of Lhasa, it is just like a mountain city. Unlike other monasteries of the Gelug Sect, the Gandain Monastery chose talented monks as its Gandain Chiba (Chief Abbot) instead of reincarnation system of the Dalai Lama or Panchen Lama. Tsongkapa, the founder of the Gandain Monastery, was succeeded by Gyachogyi, the second Chief Abbot, and until 1954, the position had been handed down to the 96th Gandain Chiba. As the ancestral monastery of the Gelug Sect, it enjoyed the highest rank in Tibetan Buddhism, especially the Gandain Chiba, ranking third following Dalai and Panchen Lamas, although the monastery had only 3,300 resident monks in history, fewer than the Zhaibung and Sera Monasteries. It was once pulled down by local people during the ten-year Culture Revolution and was rebuilt in 1980 with huge funds allocated by the central government of the People's Republic of China (PRC). Now, its main buildings such as the Grand Sutra Hall have been renovated, and there are 277 resident monks.

(2). Zhaibung Monastery

Zhaibung Monastery is the most important of the three monasteries in Lhasa. Sitting in a southern slope gully on Gebeiwoze Mountain, in the western suburbs of Lhasa, it is composed of the Gandain Phodrang (meaning Paradise Palace), Grand Sutra Hall and four Buddhist colleges, or Zhachang in Tibetan, for monks to learn Buddhist scriptures (including Losailing, Deyang, Ngaba and Gomang Zhacangs). It is a monastery with the largest scale, highest rank, and largest number of monks in the history of the Tibetan areas. During the period of the 5th Dalai Lama, he established a powerful local government headquartered in the Gandain Phodrang, hence the government was called Gandain Phodrang regime, the political power center of Tibet at that time when the Zhaibung Monastery enjoyed privileges in religious affairs. The highest number in the Zhaibung Monastery was 7,700 people, with 10,000 resident monks as its maximum permitted number. The highest position in the monastery is Chuoqin Chiba (chief abbot) and it has 427 resident monks today. The famous Shoton (Sour Milk Drinking) Festival on the 30th day of the 6th Tibetan month, started from the Zhaibung Monastery. Millions of believers and tourist swarm into the monastery for the grand and bustling fair.

(3). Sera Monastery

Sera Monastery is located on the southern slope of Serawoze Mountain in the northern suburbs of Lhasa. Of all the buildings, the most grand and magnificent are the Grand Sutra Hall and Zhacang (Buddhist colleges) buildings composed of the Meba Zhacang, the Ngaba Zhacang, the Gyi Zhacang and so on. The monastery has a rich collection of rare cultural relics, including Buddhist scriptures, Tangka paintings and Statues of Buddha. It has 327 resident monks today. It attracts an endless stream of pilgrims and sightseers.

(4). Tashilhungpo Monastery

Tashilhungpo Monastery, located in the northern suburbs of Xigaze City, is one of the six major monasteries of the Gelug Sect, and the largest one in western Tibet. It was built by Gendain Zhupa, the favorite disciple of Master Tsongkapa. He was posthumously recognized as the first Dalai Lama. Being the residential place of successive Panchen Lamas, Tashilhungpo Monastery gained a higher position in Tibetan areas. It houses 786 residential monks today. The monastery boasts the statue for Maitreya Buddha, the biggest statue of Buddha of the world, and pagodas of previous Panchen Lama that are objects of pilgrimage. With imposing halls standing in great numbers and large scale, the Tashilhungpo Monastery is regarded as a large scale Tibetan Buddhist monastery in Xigaze, and even in Tibetan areas as a whole.

(5). Tar Monastery

It lies in Huangzhong County, Qinghai Province, 26 kilometers from Xining City and birthplace of Master Tsongkapa. Constructed by local disciples in his memory, the monastery holds an important position in the fields of Tibetan Buddhism, especially in the Gelug Sect. Actually, the Tar Monastery gradually took shape from small to large scale, first as a meditation chamber built in 1560, turning into a Hall of the Buddha Maitreya 17 years later, finally forming today's scale after continuous reconstruction. The building complex is mainly composed of the Grand Sutra Hall and four Buddhist colleges (Zhacang), including the Open School Zhacang, Tantric School Zhacang, Medical Zhacang and the Time of Wheel Zhacang. It housed as many as 3,600 resident monks in its heyday. The monastery is famous for its butter sculptures, frescoes and duisui embroidery, which is listed as the Three Arts of the Tar Monastery. Architecturally speaking, it is a mixture of

Tibetan and Han palace styles, which has become a prestigious Holy Land and scenic spot in Qinghai Province for its ancient history, rich collection and convenient transportation. Housing over 500 resident monks, the Monastery holds various religious activities according to relative religious rites.

(6). Labrang Monastery

Labrang Monastery is the biggest Tibetan Buddhist Monastery in Gansu Province. Built by Jamyang Living Buddha Erwangzongze, it is located in the western suburbs of Shahe County in the Gannam Tibetan Autonomous Prefecture of Gansu Province. Sitting at the foot of a hill and besides a stream, the place is famous for its splendid scenery. Today's Labrang Monastery is mainly composed of the Grand Sutra Hall and six Buddhist colleges, namely Tiesam Lamwa, Jumaiba, Judoba, Dingker, Manba and Jido Zhacangs. The buildings are grand and imposing, housing 3,600 resident monks at their peak. Labrang Monastery is famous for its complete institutional system and generations of eminent monks, enjoying a highest prestige in the field of Tibetan Buddhism. Living Buddha Jamyang is the sixth chief abbot in the line. At present, the monastery is the biggest religious/cultural center in the Amdo Tibetan area.

7). The Shigye Sect

The Shigye sect was founded by Master Padainbasangyi. According to History and Doctrines of Different Buddhist Sects, he was born in south India, where he followed many scholars and masters to achieve high attainment in Buddhism. It was said that he went to Tibet five times and cultivated many disciples. On his last visit, he traveled to Wutai Mountain of the Han from the Tibet Autonomous Region, and during the journey his name became well known to the Han people.

The word "Shigye" literally means "put out ", so it refers to extinguishing all worries in the human world. It indicates that if one practices according to the sect's teachings and doctrines, the worries of the human world as well as their origins will be extinguished, and the existence of life and death will cease. On theory, the Shigye Sect advocates the knowledge of "nature void", while in practice in adopts a series of ascetic rituals. In 1097, Master Padainbasangyi built a monastery at Dingri. In the 14th century, the Shigye Sect owned several monasteries and furthered its development in the Tibet Autonomous Region. But, in the 15th century, it went into decline and gradually disappeared. Although the Shigye Sect had vanished as an independent sect, part of its doctrines and rituals, which were assimilated by other sects of Tibetan Buddhism, still remain.

8). The Gyoyu Sect

In Tibetan, the word "Gyoyu" has two characters, so there are also two meanings. The first meaning refers to the fact the doctrines of the sect can cut off all origins of worry in the human world; the second meaning indicates that one can attain the fields of nature void by practicing meditation.

The teachings of the Gyoyu Sect trace back to the theory of Master Padainbasangyi. So Master Tuguan Qoigyinima described the Gyoyu Sect as a branch of the Shigye Sect. It can be said that the two sects are closely related. According to *History and Doctrines of Different Buddhist Sects*, when Master Padainbasangyi entered the Tibet Autonomous Region for the third time, he imparted his teachings to Lama Gyodain Soinam and Yalhung Mareseibo, thus forming two lineages of the Gyoyu Sect. The first lineage was handed down from Yalhung Mareseibo, who imparted the teachings to his attendant Nyingba Seirong, who then handed them on to Zitun and Suntun. The successor of Zitun was Namtun, while the successors of Suntun were Gedainshemo, Zangtun and then Nyingtun. The successors of this lineage were male, so it was called the Male Lineage of the Gyoyu Sect. The second lineage was handed down by Lama Gyodain Soinam, who imparted her teachings to the female disciple Magyolhazhen. Then, the successors of this lineage were female, creating the Female Lineage of the Gyoyu Sect.

The sect come into being in the 11th century and began

to spread in the Tibetan areas. But due to its slack institutions, lax discipline, especially lack of financial support, it failed to build more monasteries. So the fate of the Gyoyu Sect was the same as that of the Shigye Sect, and in the 15th century, it had vanished. But the doctrines are mainly from *The Great Perfection Sutra*, *Collection of Tantricism*, and are recognized by masses of Buddhist disciples and followers. Therefore, many of the teachings of the Gyoyu Sect have been assimilated by other sects of Tibetan Buddhism.

At present, the foundation of the Gyoyu Sect is still maintained in the Tibetan Autonomous Region, namely Sanrikarma Monastery. This is located on a small slope in the north of Sanri County of the Shannan area. It is a middle-scale monastery, with only two stories. On the first story are the statues of Buddha Sakyamuni, Master Tsongkapa and his two close disciples. The Tibetan edition of the *Tripitaka*, including *Gangyur* and *Dangyur*, are also housed here. The second story is a sutra hall housing the statues of Master Magyolhazhen and other eminent Buddhist monks of the Gyoyu Sect. In addition, there is a cave where Master Magyolhazhen once practiced meditation, and in the cave are his statues as well as magic shoes and other offerings. It was said that in this outer cave there is another secret cave that is called the Ten Thousand Pleasure Hall, with 108 supporting pillars, where Master Magyolhazhen secretly practiced meditation. In 1086, Master Magyolhazhen built Sanrikarma Monastery as the foundation of her religious activities. Now, after hundreds of years of wind and rain, the monastery still not only disseminates the teachings of the Gyoyu Sect, but also spreads that of the Gelug and Kargyu sects as well as other sects of Tibetan Buddhism. People can feel the existence of the spirit of the Gyoyu Sect through the deep content and particular form of the Sanrikarma Monastery.

9). The Bhulu Sect

The Bhulu Sect, also known as the Shalu Sect, was only a small sect founded by Master Pertain Renqencho (1290-

1364), so it has been suggested that it would be more appropriate to call it a school rather than a sect. Whatever, Master Pertain Renqencho was a real famous figure in the history of Tibetan Buddhism. He was born in a small village near Chopo of the U-Tsang region, and his father was an eminent monk of the Nyingma Sect, while his mother had high Buddhist achievements. Hence, the boy received good education. When he was five or six years old, he began to follow his mother to study *Wisdom Sutra before Dying*, *Time Wheel Sutra of Ksitigarbha* and other Buddhist scriptures; One year later, he went to Master Chopoba, under whom he studied *Mahayana Bodhisattva's Resolution*; At the age of eight, he studied under his grandfather Cechen Nyingbo *Realization of the Great Perfection*, *Dharma Realm of Great Perfection* and other Tantric elements of the Nyingma Sect; later, he listened to the explanations of *Tantricism of the Shigye Sect*, *Trema (concealed treasure) of Master Padmasambhava* and so on. Based on his good education, Purdain mastered teachings of the Nyingma Sect in his childhood and was called a "child prodigy" at that time. But he dissatisfied with what he had learned, and at the age of 17, he started to study "Three Tibetan" and "Five Classics " under many famous scholars and monks. During that time, he learned all the Buddhist monastic disciplines and teachings of practicing meditation. One year later, he was formally ordained as an Sramanera (Junior Monk), and then, at the age of 23, he received ordination as a Bhiksu. What he had learned and practiced strictly followed the orders and rituals of the orthodox theory of Buddhism. So, he was not only a learned scholar, but also had solid and profound knowledge of Buddhism. Around the age of 30, he had fully grasped all the teachings and rituals of various sects of Tibetan Buddhism, such as the Nyingma, Sakya, Kardam, Kargyu, Shigye, and Gyoyu sects. What's more, his attainments and ideology of Buddhism was mature and complete. From then on, Master Purdain rose to be a shining pearl in the field of Tibetan Buddhism. He set out to lecture of profound doctrines of Tibetan Buddhism, such as The Great Perfection Sutra, Buddhist Logic, Collection of Mahayana Abhidharma and so on. Meanwhile, hie high reputation started to spread among his followers in the Tibetan areas.

In 1320, at the invitation of Kushang Zhaba Gyaincain, the feudal lord of Shalu in the southeast of the Xigaze area, Master Purdain went to Shalu Monastery to serve as its chief Abbot. He spared no pains to lecture on Buddhist scriptures to the resident monks as well as visiting monks and scholars. Due to his great knowledge, many monks and followers of Buddhism were attracted to the monastery. Soon, the resident monks rose to 2,800, and four sutra colleges were formed. Shalu Monastery, thus, was famous in the Tibetan areas. Master Purdain also wrote many books. In 1322, he finished the famous work on Buddhist history, *History on Buddhism by Purdain*, and later he compiled the directory of *Dangyur*, which was included in the Tibetan edition of the Tripitaka. Those two works exerted great influence on the development of Tibetan Buddhism in later generations. According to the woodcut edition in the period of the 13th Dalai, the works of Master Purdain amounted to 28 caskets, over 200 types, which is rare in the Tibetan areas.

As the Shalu Monastery was heavily reliant on the prestige of Master Purdain, after his death it lost influence. However, its construction style has peculiar charm, combining the construction arts of the Han and Tibetan. It boasts ancient frescos as well as complete and various relics and historical books. Besides the Great Sutra Hall in the central area, there are also stand eight halls of Buddha, namely the Hall of Silver Nimble Stupa, the North and South Halls, the Hall of Buddha Infinite Life, the Hall of Horse-necked Vajra, the Hall of Protection Deities, the Hall of Gyaingung, and the Hall of Meditation. At present, it houses 57 resident monks, among of whom only four are elderly.

Today, the monastery still holds many Buddhist ceremonies and various religious rituals. The main activities are: Time Wheel Ceremony, held three times every year, with the first from the 10th to the 23rd day of the seventh month of the Tibetan calendar, the second from the 10th to the 23rd day of the eighth month of the Tibetan calendar, the third in the ninth month of the Tibetan calendar; Ceremony of Bdemchogrdorje, held from the 14th to the 15th of the 12th month of the Tibetan calendar; Ceremony of Vaisravana, held from the 10th to the 23rd day of the fifth month of the Tibetan calendar; various ceremonies of Vajra Realm and other ceremonies.

Besides Shalu Monastery, in Nyimo County of the Tibetan Autonomous Region there is another monastery of the Bhulu Sect called Naro Monastery. But it is a small-scale monastery with little influence. The Bhulu Sect has lost its power as sect, but as a school, many Buddhist monks and followers still would like to mention it and talk about it.

A mosque in Lhasa.

Islam

People through ages commonly have held the view that Tibetans by and large have worshipped Buddhism. However, although Tibetan Buddhism does indeed dominate people's religious life in the Land of Snows, we can find several sacred halls of Islam. At present, there are four small or large mosques in the Tibet Autonomous Region, and we need to go back to the 8th Century to trace their origins.

Available historical records show that, as early as the period of the Tubo Kingdom in the 8th century, Tibetans were associated with Muslim businessmen from Arabia. In the 11th century, Islam flourished in the Kashmir area to the west of the Tibet Autonomous Region, which made it more convenient for Muslims going to Lhasa to engage in business. In the 14th century, Kashmiri Muslims began to settle in Lhasa City and gradually assembled to form a new national communication. Tibetans called them Khache, which means in Tibetan "Muslim". With the almost total triumph of Buddhism in Tibet, especially in Lhasa, Islam eventually failed to establish deep roots in the city. In the reign of the 5th Dalai Lama, the Gelug Sect of Tibetan Buddhism grew vigorously, and Kashmiri Islamism was hindered in expanding its influence. As a result, the tradition of Islam was only followed by businessmen and butchers catering for Muslims in Tibet, which was small and unitary in terms of followers.

But to some degree, Tibetans depended on Muslims and for two major reasons. First, market and business activities relied on Muslims, and, secondly, cities and towns of the Tibetan areas need special butchers to kill animals. As Tibetans, long influenced by Tibetan Buddhism, they have little interest in business and are especially reluctant to kill living things because of religious taboo. Therefore, due to social requirements, Islam in the end managed to take roots in the Tibetan areas.

Historical records show that the first mosque in Lhasa City was built in the period of Emperor Kangxi of the Qing Dynasty. It was located at today's Hebalhin in the Chengguan district of Lhasa City (300 meters east of Barkor Street), and was called the Great Mosque of Lhasa. At first, it was only a small mosque and only covered an area of 200 square meters. Later, it was renovated and extended in 1793, when troops dispatched by the Qing government succeeded in suppressing a rebellion by Koerkars. It indirectly indicates that there were quite a number of Muslims among those Qing troops from the Han areas. The inscribed board that reads Dignity and Orthodox Religion kept in the mosque dates back to the 30th year of Emperor Qianlong, namely 1766, which shows that Muslims from the Han area lived in Lhasa City at that time. Unfortunately, the mosque was burnt down by rebels when several upper-class national separatists launched an armed rebellion against the Chinese central government. In 1960, it was reconstructed, and in 1978, after the Third Plenary Session of the eleventh Central Committee of the Communist Party of China (CPC), the monastery was further renovated. In 1985, on the occasion of the 20th anniversary of the foundation of the Tibet Autonomous Region, central government presented the Great Mosque of Lhasa with an inscribed board that reads "the Ancient Mosque", which now hangs over the building.

A mosque in Lhasa.

 Tibetan Religions

At present, the Great Mosque of Lhasa covers an area of 2,600 square meters, with a floor area of 1,300 square meters, with an outer gate, outer court, dormitory, minarets, church, bathroom and so on. The gate faces north and evokes an atmosphere of somber silence. The minaret is a four-story watchtower 13 meters tall and 13 meters in circumference, and it is an exquisite building made of stone and wood. The church, the most imposing building of all, stands on a platform that is one meter above the ground. The church covers a floor area of 285 square miters, with the gate facing east and 13 pillars inside supporting the building. The whole church is permeated with an atmosphere of elegance and silence. In the hall, the floor is covered with large carpet and on the wall of west side hangs a tapestry of the Mecca Kabala, while on the north side stands a pulpit for the Ahung to lecture. Now, the abbot of the Great Mosque of Lhasa is Ahung Heisam, who presides over the salat (congregational prayers) every Jom'a Day (Friday) and lectures on doctrine in Arabian first, then explaining it in detail in Tibetan.

Besides the Great Mosque of Lhasa, there is another one called the Small Mosque of Lhasa by contemporary people. This is said to have been built in the 1920's, and is situated 200 meters southeast of Barkor Street. Historical records show it was built for non-native Muslims, mainly businessmen from Kashmir, Ladakh, Nepal and so on. Although it only has a floor area of 130 square meters, the mosque is characteristic for its Tibetan style of construction.

At present, Muslims who stay or reside at the city of Lhasa not only possess religious places where they freely practice religious activities, but also have two Muslim cemeteries, respectively located at Tortiko in the northern suburbs and at Gyichalhutin in the western suburbs, both built according to Islamic tradition and customs. The famous ceremony of "hands-eating rice festival" for Muslims, held regularly every August, is held at the Tortilo cemetery. Muslims live there in the open countryside, during which time the Koran, the holy scripture of Islam, will be discussed by the Ahung and other important rituals such as congregational prayers will be held at the same time. In addition, since 1984, some Muslims go on pilgrimage to Mecca.

Besides the two mosques in Lhasa, there are also two others respectively in Xigaze and Chenguan of Qamdo County.

How many adherents of Muslim live in the Tibetan Autonomous Region? In 1903 there were altogether over 200 Muslims from Ladakh or the western regions of the People's Republic of China, who were engaged mainly in business activities. Apart from the mosque, they also had a Muslim restaurant, managed by Muslims from the western regions of China. In 1936, the number of Muslims from Ladakh alone increased to between 200 and 300. Most of them wore Tibetan dress, but maintained their tradition of wearing a turban or veil. In terms of food, they liked to eat meat, zanba, and drink tea milk or butter milk. It can be learned that although those Muslims still kept their characteristic features, they had been Tibetanized: in terms of living customs. They had assimilated much from Tibetans and had many similarities; in terms of language.

In 1964, there are 1,195 Muslims in the Tibetan Autonomous Region, and in 1982, the number grew to 1,788. In 1992, there are altogether 2,907 Muslims living in the region, around 2,000 in Lhasa alone, rising to today's figure of around 4,000.

The church of Roman Catholithism of Yamgyin, where Father Lhurenti is reading mass.

Roman Catholicism

In the Tibetan Autonomous Region, besides the Bon religion, Tibetan Buddhism, and Islam, there is a branch of Christianity, Roman Catholicism, which has certain influence in limited area. Historical records show Catholicism was introduced through India into western Tibet in the Ngari area, where, through the ages, diverse cultures have merged, because it is located to south of Xinjiang and borders on Kashmir on the west and Nepal on the southwest. Western missionaries took advantage of this geographical advantage to spread Catholicism to Tibet. In 1624, Father Andrade and the missionary Macques, after a hard trek, reached the Zebolhung area, which is located in the valley of the Shangchan River of the Ngari area. Seeing it to be a good place, with pleasant weather, abundant water and fertile soil, they decided to settle down to spread their religion. As their first effort, they presented expensive gifts to the king of Guge, the ruling power of the Ngari area at that time. They succeeded to establishing good relations with the ruler, and, in 1626, at Zebolhung, with his permission and support, they established the first church in Tibet. Unfortunately, four years later, the church was demolished by supporters of Tibetan Buddhism, totally stopping the spread of Catholicism.

In eastern Tibet, in the Xigaze area, Western missionaries also tried to establish a base for Catholicism. In 1628, the missionaries Kacella, and Cabral entered the Xigaze area from Bhutan. They managed to win the permission of the local leader, Zangbarhan, and began to build a church and preach. However, they failed to conquer the hostility of monks and followers of Tibetan Buddhism, and three years later, they had to abandon their efforts.

Thereafter, ceaseless efforts were made to spread Catholicism in Lhasa. According to historical records, in 1661, Catholic missionaries went to Lhasa for the first time and stayed about two months; after that, missionaries from different organizations went in succession in 1709, 1714, 1716, 1718, 1720, 1727, 1741 and so on to Lhasa to try to spread their religious beliefs. After their concerted efforts, in 1721, they succeeded in building a small church. Yet, 20 years later, there wasn't a single Tibetan convert, only some believers from Nepal, Kashmir, and the Han areas. Later, 26 Tibetans, all of whom were servants and maids of the Western missionaries or children, were persuaded to receive baptism in the church. However, in 1745, the missionaries were expelled by the local government and their church demolished, due to the total incompatibility between Catholicism with Tibetan Buddhism. As the result, after a century of efforts by Western missionaries in Tibet, Catholicism failed to take root and had to admit failure.

After the 19th century, Western missionaries no longer made their way into the central areas of Tibet, and instead turned to some Tibetan areas of Sichuan, Qinghai and Yunnan provinces. But they encountered the same hostility from believers in Tibetan Buddhism. At that time, those Western missionaries spread their religious beliefs mainly on Lhitam, Bartam, Tagyanlho and other remote Tibetan areas. Many violent incidents took place between adherents of Tibetan Buddhism and the missionaries, finally forcing the latter to withdraw. However, a

Father Lhurenti, the first Tibetan Father graduated from Chinese Institute of Divinity Studies

161

The church of Roman Catholithism of Yamgyin, characteristics of a Tibetan construction style.

Catholic church stands majestic in Yamgyin Naxi County of Mangkam County in the Qamdo area of the Tibetan Autonomous Region, a remote area near Bartam of Sichuan Province and Teqin of Yunnan Province. Available records do not reveal the exact time when it was constructed. The general view is that it was built in 1862, although this remains in dispute. Another story is that, in 1879, a French missionary went to the Yamgyin area, reaching Bartam the following year to meet with Father Biert. In 1887, he was driven out of Bartam and traveled toward Tagyanlho, and then Yamgyin. In the end he died at Yamgyin in August of 1894. Whatever, after over two centuries of efforts, those Western missionaries finally managed to plant a small tree of Catholicism in the remote area of the Tibetan Autonomous Region. Today, the small tree is not withered, but grows with luxuriant foliage and spreading branches, which is a kind of posthumous consolation for those Western missionaries who made such strenuous efforts to spread Catholicism. At present, in Yamgyin there is a small church, the only Catholic church in the Tibetan Autonomous Region, with a congregation of 560 Tibetans.